Hey, Who Is That Man?

The introduction that will change your life

Barry St. Clair

This book is designed for your personal reading
pleasure and profit. It is also designed for group
study. A leader's guide, with visual aids (Son-
Power Multiuse Transparency Masters) and Rip-
Offs (student activity booklets) are available from
your local Christian bookstore or from the
publisher.

VICTOR BOOKS

a division of SP Publications, Inc.

WHEATON, ILLINOIS 60187

Offices also in Fullerton, California • Whitby, Ontario, Canada • Amersham-on-the-Hill, Bucks, England

Library of Congress Catalog Card Number: 82-80893
ISBN: 0-88207-583-7

VICTOR BOOKS
A division of SP Publications, Inc.
Box 1825 • Wheaton, Ill. • 60187

*Rick Biesiadecki
3329 Summit
Turf Lane*

What You'll Be Reading

*Snellville, Ga.
30278*

The Man 6
1 Blind Dates and Introductions 7
2 Down to Earth 18
3 Bridging the Gap 28
4 The Resurrection—Rip-off or Reality? 37
5 Knowing Jesus 52
6 Jesus Is Lord! 65
7 Lord of Priorities 76
8 Lord of Attitudes 89
9 Lord Over Temptation 100
10 Lord of Love, Sex, and Dating 112
11 Lord of Character 123
12 Lord of All 137

To my wife Carol . . .

She keeps me growing
in the Man.

The Man

There once was a man a long time ago,
standing alone against the status quo.
He worked with his hands and grew tall and strong;
he worked with his mind sorting right from wrong.
He was sure of his mission and he spoke loud and
    clear,
and he got every eye and got every ear.

But some didn't like him, it was plain to see,
'cause he put them down for their hypocrisy.
The idea of loving was drastic and new,
and bucking the crowd was just too much to do.
Things haven't changed from those days of old;
they still try to make him fit into their mold.

There isn't a man or a woman too low,
but what he would love them and help them to know
that if they would dare to prove him on out,
he'd slam down all their fear and all of their doubts.
It's not the easiest choice you can make;
it's playing for keeps with a whole lot at stake.

Now you can't go pointing at what others do,
'cause it's a personal thing, strictly between him and
    you.
And if you're really wanting to give life a pull,
alive to your fingertips, brimming and full,
then give him a try, going out on a limb.
You'll never know life till you really know him.

—Ralph Carmichael

1

Blind Dates and Introductions

My first blind date was a wipeout. Two weeks into my freshman year in college I had joined a fraternity. I didn't know any of the local girls so I asked my fraternity brothers to get a date for me. The college was an all male school, but my fraternity brothers knew girls from a girls school nearby.

When the guys told me about the date they had lined up for me, I started getting excited. They said she was absolutely great—fine looking, wonderful personality, everything. It was going to be a super evening.

My date was for 8 P.M. About 3 o'clock that afternoon, I started getting ready. I scrubbed myself in the shower for over an hour. Then I put on deodorant—about four different kinds. My armpits squeaked when I moved. I was so hyped by this time that I splashed on half of a bottle of aftershave.

At 8 o'clock my fraternity brothers and I drove over to the dormitory where we were to meet our dates. I was as nervous as a long-tailed cat in a roomful of rocking chairs. I tried to be cool. But the sweaty palms, the shortness of breath, the dry lips gave away my excitement. I waited for my date in the lobby of her dormitory. My friends were there too, waiting for their dates, and ready to point mine out when she came downstairs.

Finally this gorgeous girl came down. *She must be the one!* I thought as my heartbeat accelerated. But she wasn't. Another good-looking girl came down, then another. Each time, I thought, *this must be the one!* But no way. They were my "friends'" dates!

Finally someone came down the stairs who looked like a cross between the dorm house-mother and the janitor. That was *my* date! Needless to say, I was disappointed. And I could soon tell that my date wasn't overly impressed with me either.

Now really, the girl wasn't that bad looking. In fact, we might have had an enjoyable evening if I hadn't built up so many false expectations. But because I had allowed my imagination to run away with me, I probably would have felt let down regardless of who had come down those stairs. If only my friends had told me what my date was really like.

It was obvious that the girl had been given a lot of false information about me too. What was to have been a super evening turned out to be a super flop.

People often build up unrealistic expectations about blind dates. What people expect from Jesus Christ is often unrealistic as well. Yet those expectations affect the way a person thinks about Him—sometimes forever.

The way I met my blind date is the way I think some people are introduced to Jesus. They have been told certain things about Him that have given them all sorts of wrong impressions.

But there is a difference between the wrong impressions I had about my blind date and the wrong impressions people have about Jesus. The difference usually is that people hear all *bad* things about Him when the truth is that He is absolutely *good*. Wrong impressions make it hard for people to appreciate the real Jesus.

Wrong Impressions

Wrong impression #1: "God is out to get you!" Many people think of God as the Celestial Scrooge who sits in the sky with His big stick. Every time you get out of line—*whack! whack! whack!*—He clobbers you. For that reason they're afraid to commit their lives to Jesus. They think that if they do, He'll make them go to "Bunga Bunga Land" and hand out tracts on the street corner.

Wrong impression #2: "Following Jesus means you're a wimp." Many people "know" Jesus as some pale, weak, religious leader who died 2,000 years ago. They assume that following Him means wearing a dorky-looking suit and tie, carrying a 50-pound King James Bible under your arm, and hanging a sign on your back that says "Walk on me, I'm a Christian wimp."

Wrong impression #3: "Following Jesus means keeping tons of rules." Many high school students have the impression that Christianity is a list of rules—a collection of do's and don'ts: "Take the

10 things you like most and stop doing them. And take the 10 things you hate most and start doing them." But that's not what it means to follow Jesus Christ.

Wrong impression #4: "Following Jesus is an emotional high." Others get the impression that being a Christian is one big emotional experience—that if a person cries enough and gets the right "warm feeling in his heart," then he's a Christian. Becoming a Christian *can* mean having some strong emotional feelings, but believe me, it's more than just emotions.

Wrong impression #5: "Following Jesus means going to church." Another commonly held wrong impression is that God lives in a box called the church, and every Sunday, people go there to meet with Him. Going to church is important, but God doesn't live in a church building. He's out in the world where people live, work, eat, and sleep. Going into a church doesn't make you a Christian any more than going into a garage makes you a car.

Having the wrong impression can produce disastrous consequences. We need to know Jesus for who He really is—and not reject Him because of a wrong impression.

An Introduction That Worked

Fortunately for me, I've had other introductions that were better than the one which accompanied my blind date. For example, there's the first time I saw Carol. I walked into the school library and looked around for a place to sit. I looked over to the right, and there she was—the finest looking lady I had ever seen. Right away I knew I wanted to meet her. I took a "check out" position behind a bookshelf, pushed some books around, and peeked through.

The problem was that she was with another guy. I decided the best way to meet her was to walk right up and start talking to the guy she was with. He was a nice guy. And because he was so nice, he had no choice but to introduce me.

Carol and I started talking. And then I kept on talking with her . . . and talking . . . and talking. For all I know, the guy who introduced us is still back there sitting in the library.

The next night I asked Carol out for a "study" date. That's a date in which you come to the library, study for five minutes, and then leave. We went out and talked some more. Over the months, the relationship developed. Then came an engagement, and a marriage, and later, three kids.

The way I got to know Carol was totally different from the way I met that girl on the blind date. Following our introduction, Carol and I established a dynamic relationship. The difference? We started right—no false expectations, no wrong impressions, no rotten introductions.

Starting Right

Starting right with Jesus requires a proper introduction to Him. It requires an understanding of who Jesus really is.

John, in his Gospel, introduced Jesus as the One who was with God the Father from the very beginning (John 1:1). Jesus' coming to earth wasn't a last-minute decision on God's part. In fact, the Old Testament makes 300 references to the coming of Christ. That indicates that God had, from the beginning, planned to send His Son Jesus to earth so people could know who God is through His Son. Jesus Himself said, "Anyone who has seen Me has seen the Father" (John 14:9).

John said, "the Word became flesh and lived for a while among us. We have seen His glory, the glory of the one and only Son, who came from the Father, full of grace and truth" (John 1:14). So Jesus came and identified with us. Jesus literally became a man.

Luke said, "Jesus grew in wisdom and stature and in favor with God and man" (Luke 2:52). Jesus grew up like any other child of His day. He went through His teen years like all of us. There was probably a time when His legs looked too long and His feet too big and His voice sounded squeaky as it began to change. He may have had complexion problems like most of us.

And Jesus grew up to be a man. He was entirely *human*. When He got hungry, He had to eat. When He got thirsty, He wanted something to drink. If His sandals rubbed His toes, He got blisters.

Contrary to some people's wrong impressions, Jesus was a man's man. He was a carpenter whose hard work calloused His hands and hardened His muscles. He didn't worry about getting a little dirt under His fingernails. He was a man whom real men can identify with. If you don't know that kind of Jesus, then you don't know the Jesus of the Bible.

Jesus came to identify with us personally. The

Apostle Paul described Him as "the image of the invisible God" (Colossians 1:15). In other words, Jesus was the visible expression of the invisible God. He came so that we could *see* who God is. When we look at the person of Jesus Christ that's exactly who we see—God.

Running around in my house while I write this is an eight-year-old named Scott. If you took pictures of him made at different ages in his life and placed them beside pictures of me made when I was the same ages, you would hardly be able to tell who was who. Scott's got puffy spots under his eyes just like I did. He's got a big mouth that curves all over his face just like I did. He's got blond hair like mine was. He's the spitting image of his dad. And Jesus is the spitting image of who God is!

Powerful Claims

Jesus Himself claimed to be God's Son sent from heaven. Notice how Jesus introduced Himself. He said, "All authority in heaven and on earth has been given to Me" (Matthew 28:18). God not only sent Him, *He gave Him all authority*—the delegated power of God.

On the busiest intersection of a large city stands a man wearing a blue uniform, a beaked cap, and a whistle around his neck. When that policeman directs a semitrailer to turn right, it turns right. But if a senior at your school goes out there wearing a T-shirt and jeans, and blows a whistle, he'll probably have a VW bug leave tread marks on his face. The policeman may have no more physical

power than the student. But he has the authority—
the delegated power of the police department.

Jesus has God's authority. That's why He could
make the claims that He made. Never mind, for
now, what others say about Jesus. Let's check out
some of His claims and see what He said about
Himself:

*Jesus claimed to have power to forgive people's
sins*. One day when Jesus was teaching in a friend's
home, a crippled man was brought to Him and
lowered into the crowded room through a hole his
friends had made in the roof. Jesus not only healed
the man but told him, "your sins are forgiven"
(Mark 2:5).

Later Jesus told the crowd, " 'Which is easier:
to say to the paralytic, "Your sins are forgiven," or
to say, "Get up, take your mat and walk"? But that
you may know that the Son of Man has authority
on earth to forgive sins. . . .' He said to the paralytic, 'I tell you, get up, take your mat and go
home' " (Mark 2:9-10).

Jesus claimed that God was His Father. When
the Jewish leaders criticized Him for healing on
the Sabbath Day, Jesus said, "My Father is always
at His work to this very day, and I, too, am working . . . He who does not honor the Son does not
honor the Father who sent Him" (John 5:17, 23).

Jesus claimed to be the only way to God. He
said, "I am the way and the truth and the life. No
one comes to the Father except through Me." (John
14:6).

Jesus claimed to be eternal. To a group of skep-
tical Jewish leaders, Jesus proclaimed, "Your father
Abraham rejoiced at the thought of seeing My day;
he saw it and was glad" (John 8:56). When the

Jews protested that it was impossible for Jesus to have known someone who died hundreds of years earlier, Jesus replied, "before Abraham was born, I am!" (John 8:58)

Jesus claimed to be God in human form. "I and the Father are one," He stated (John 10:30). And when Jesus' disciple Philip asked, "Lord, show us the Father," Jesus told him plainly, "Anyone who has seen Me has seen the Father" (John 14:9).

Don't let anyone fool you. Jesus claimed to be more than just another good teacher or holy man— like Buddha or Mohammed. He claimed to be a whole lot more. The question is, are His claims true? Can He back them up?

Proof Positive

A story is told about a young man named Russ who went bear hunting with some friends. The group was discussing who was the best bear hunter. Russ got carried away and blurted out, "I can catch a bear with my bare hands!"

"We don't believe you," his fellow hunters replied. Embarrassed, Russ grabbed his coat and stalked out into a blinding snowstorm.

Several hours later Russ' friends were worried about him. They were watching for him through the window of the cabin where they were staying. Finally they saw a tiny dot coming through the snow toward the cabin with another tiny dot behind it. They could hear someone yelling faintly, "Help! Open the door! Open the door!"

As the dots got closer, Russ' friends could see that it was Russ and a huge grizzly bear just inches behind him. Russ was still yelling, "Open the door! Open the door!" Closer and closer he came, with the bear right behind him. His friends swung the door open. Right at the door, Russ suddenly jumped aside and the huge bear came crashing into the cabin. "H-h-h-here," Russ stammered, "you guys skin this one—I'm going back for another one."

Russ made big claims, but he couldn't back them up. Throughout history people have made big claims about having "special relationships" with God. But only Jesus Christ can fully back up every claim He has ever made! It's one thing to claim to be God. It's another thing to actually *prove* it:

Jesus said, "I am the bread of life" (John 6:35). Jesus could say that because He had just performed a miracle to feed over 5,000 people (John 6:5-13).

Jesus said, "I am the light of the world" (John 8:12). Shortly after He said this, He restored sight to a blind man. At least nine blind people in the New Testament were healed by Jesus. These weren't people who were a little nearsighted or who needed their contact lenses adjusted either—these people were totally blind.

Jesus said, "I am the resurrection and the life" (John 11:25). Jesus made this statement near the grave of His friend Lazarus who had been dead for four days and whose body had already begun to smell. At Jesus' command, Lazarus got up and walked out of the grave *alive*.

Jesus said He would rise from the dead after three days (Matthew 16:21). Three days after He had been nailed to the cross, Jesus burst out of the grave!

Your Introduction

Have you been properly introduced to Jesus Christ? If you have, you can get to know Him better in the following chapters. If you haven't, ask Him to introduce Himself to you as you read this book.

The next three chapters take a closer look at *why* Jesus came and died, and examine the critical question, "Did He really rise from the dead?" As you read, remember one thing: If Jesus is who He claimed to be—the Son of God who lived a sinless life, died on the cross for the world's sins, and rose from the dead—you ought to follow Him at any cost. Think about it.

2

Down to Earth

I'm a killer. I don't want to be, but I can't help it. Almost without knowing what I'm doing, I bring destruction and death to an innocent, peace-loving family.

It's like this. The pavement in my driveway has some cracks in it. Ants have made an anthill under the concrete slabs. I see them crawling in and out over the ridge of dirt they've built up around the entrance to their nest. Nearly every time I leave my house, it's doomsday for the ant family.

It's a terrible sight. I back out of my garage and look back to see all these little guys strewn across my driveway. They've been crunched. A few of them have gotten caught in between the tire treads and they're hanging on for dear life. The rest of the survivors are running around frantically. They have no idea what hit them. And I'm wondering if I should call the paramedics or what.

I could try telling the ants to move their home about three feet to one side or the other. I might even get down on my hands and knees and shout at the little critters to move. Or I could try blowing them to one side, or sticking a match to several of them to get them moving in the right direction.

But the fact is I'll never be able to communicate with those ants. The only way I could make them understand me would be for me to become one of them.

That's what Jesus did! He came to earth because God wanted to communicate with us on a level we could understand. Paul wrote this about Jesus: He is "the visible expression of the invisible God" (Colossians 1:15, PH). John wrote: "The Word became flesh and dwelt among us, and we beheld His glory, glory as of the only begotten from the Father, full of grace and truth" (John 1:14, NASB).

The word John used for *dwelt* means literally, "pitched a tent." Jesus "pitched His tent" among us so we could get to know God and understand what He wanted to communicate to us.

In his letter to the Galatians, Paul summed up why Christ came: "When the time had fully come, God sent His Son, born of a woman, born under Law, to redeem those under Law, that we might receive the full rights of sons. Because you are sons, God sent the Spirit of His Son into our hearts, the Spirit who calls out, 'Abba, Father.' So you are no longer a slave, but a son; and since you are a son, God has made you also an heir" (Galatians 4:4-7).

This passage tells us three truths about the purpose of Christ's coming to earth—three things God gave us in Jesus Christ: a *cradle*, a *cross*, and a *crown*.

A Child Is Born

You can't imagine the excitement that filled our house when our first child was born. When we found out we were going to be parents, Carol and I went crazy with excitement.

We bought a baby bed and a new chest of drawers for the nursery. We didn't know whether the nursery should be pink for a girl or blue for a boy, so we compromised and painted the room yellow. We bought a big supply of Pampers.

Finally the day came for our baby to be born. Carol woke me up in the middle of the night to tell me it was time. We got dressed hurriedly and headed for the hospital. I had the camera ready and took pictures of Carol going out the door, getting into the car, riding in the wheelchair at the hospital, and checking into her room.

The most exciting part started about 4 o'clock that afternoon when Carol and I entered the delivery room. We had decided that if the baby was a girl she would be "Katie" and if a boy he would be "Scott." Carol worked at bringing the baby into the world. Suddenly the nurse began to yell, "It's a Scott! It's a Scott!"

My first reaction was: *What is she talking about?* Then it hit me. I'm a father! I have a Scott!

That's how exciting it must have been when Jesus was born, right? Wrong.

His Cradle

A tired young mother-to-be, probably still a teenager, made an exhausting journey to Bethlehem from Nazareth and arrived in the overcrowded, dusty town just when her baby was due.

Imagine what it must have been like for Joseph and Mary—a young couple engaged to be married, and she turns up pregnant. On top of that, Joseph wasn't the father. Joseph had thought of breaking up with Mary, till God sent a messenger to tell him that the child had been conceived by the Holy Spirit (Matthew 1:18-21).

Then the news came that Joseph and Mary would have to go to Bethlehem for the Roman census. They had no choice but to go.

They arrived in Bethlehem, which must have looked that night like the halls of a high school when classes are changing. Everybody was in town for the census. The place must have been a madhouse.

Joseph was told that there were no vacancies at the inn. When he explained to the innkeeper that the baby was on the way, the best the innkeeper could offer was a stable, probably a cave behind the inn.

There was no new baby bed or furniture. No freshly painted room. No Pampers. Nothing—but a cold, smelly stable. If God hadn't announced the occasion to some shepherds in the fields nearby, no one would have noticed the tiny, wiggling form that Mary wrapped in cloth and placed in a manger. What a way for the Son of God to enter the world!

I can imagine Mary caressing the tiny hands of her nursing child—hands that one day would reach out and touch blind men's eyes and make them see. In that dark, cold cave that night, the tiny feet that would one day walk the hills of Galilee kicked softly in the manger straw. They were the same feet that would one day turn toward Jerusalem to face death on a cross.

The squeaky noises from His mouth were the first earthly sounds of the One who would one day say, "I am the way and the truth and the life. No one comes to the Father except through Me" (John 14:6). It was that tiny voice that would announce, "I am the resurrection and the life. He who believes in Me . . . will never die" (John 11:25-26).

This tiny baby was God's Son, the link between a loving Father and a lost world. He was God becoming a man to communicate God's love to a people who could never understand it any other way.

Second Birth

The same God who brought about the miracle of Jesus' birth wants to bring about new birth in every person.

"I've already been born!" someone says. Good thinking. But Jesus says He wants us to be born a second time. He wants us to be born *spiritually* just as we were born physically.

A man named Nicodemus asked Jesus how to have eternal life. Jesus told him, "Unless a man is born again, he cannot see the kingdom of God" (John 3:3).

A lot of people have wrong ideas about what it means to be born again. They claim to have experienced new birth, but their lives remain the same. Let's get it straight. Being born again does not mean becoming part of a youth group, joining a church, "turning over a new leaf," or becoming religious.

When Jesus told Nicodemus that he needed to be born again, He was talking about entering into a dynamic, personal relationship with the living God. He was talking about opening one's life to let Jesus enter it and change it so that it would never be the same again.

"To all who received Him, to those who believed in His name, He gave the right to become children of God" (John 1:12). A person is born again when he receives Jesus into his life.

An even clearer picture emerges from Revelation 3:20: "Here I am! I stand at the door and knock. If anyone hears My voice and opens the door, I will go in and eat with him, and he with Me."

Jesus stands at the door of your life and knocks. If you let Him in to live inside you, you are born again. If you don't open the door of your life, then you are not born again. It's that simple.

Jesus won't beat the door down either. He is a gentleman. If you don't want to open it, that's your choice. But if you do open it, He promises to come in.

His Cross

I asked a friend named Rick, "Suppose someone came along and kidnapped your girlfriend Debbie, then sent you a note saying that if you paid so much money, Debbie would be set free. How much would you be willing to pay to get her back? Ten dollars?"

"Sure," Rick said.

"What about $25?"

"Yeah, sure."

"What about $100? $500? $1,000? How about a million?"

"Sure, if I could get hold of that much, I'd pay a million dollars," Rick replied.

In regard to an even bigger ransom deal, the Apostle Paul wrote, "God sent His Son, born of a woman, born under Law, to redeem those under Law" (Galatians 4:4-5). The word *redeem* means to buy back, to make an exchange for something you consider of great value. Paying the ransom, as Rick was willing to pay to get Debbie back from the kidnappers, is the idea expressed in the word *redeem*.

Mankind was captured by sin, headed straight to hell. Christ came to buy us back. And at what a price! If we want to know how much God was willing to pay to buy us back, all we have to do is look at Jesus on the cross.

Often when we think of the baby Jesus lying in a manger, we think of the bright star that stood over Bethlehem shining down on Him to point the wise men to where He was. But it might be more to the point to think of the shadow of a *cross* looming over that manger in Bethlehem.

Imagine the agony and pain in God's heart as He and Jesus counseled in heaven over man's captivity to sin. Imagine the Father's anguish when He decided what the price would be—that His only Son should come to earth to be spat on, beaten, mistreated, scourged, mocked, and nailed to a cross.

I have three children, and I love them dearly.

I also love the young people to whom I minister week after week. But I'm glad no one has ever asked me to give the life of one of my children so that someone in my youth group could live. I love those students, but none of them mean so much to me that I could offer my own child to die for them.

But God willingly gave His only Son to die for us so that we might be brought back to Him. He loved us that much. I'm convinced that if people really see how much God loves them, as He demonstrated on the cross, they won't keep living as though Jesus never died.

How *should* we respond to the fact that Jesus paid the price of buying us back with His own life? Paul wrote, "Therefore, I urge you, brothers, in view of God's mercy, to offer your bodies as living sacrifices, holy and pleasing to God—which is your spiritual worship" (Romans 12:1).

The same word that is used here of Christ's sacrifice is used of *our* sacrifice. Jesus died on the cross for us. He wants us, in turn, to die to ourselves.

What does it mean to *die to ourselves?* To answer that question, we must ask what it is within each of us that raises its ugly head and says, "Do it *your* way."

What is it in your life? Is it your temper, your attitude toward parents, your friends, your attitude toward material things, your sex life?

Jesus asks that we offer our lives to Him—all that we are, the good and the bad in us. Instead of "doing it our way," Jesus asks that we let Him take control. As we *die* to ourselves, He will *live* through us.

His Crown

Imagine being the son or daughter of a king. Imagine getting everything you wanted: 500 new record albums, 100 new shirts, 50 pairs of new jeans, 10 TR7s. That's what it might be like if you were the son or daughter of a wealthy monarch. Listen. . . .

God calls us Christians His sons and daughters. Remember Galatians 4:6-7? "Because you are sons, God sent the Spirit of His Son into our hearts, the Spirit who calls out, 'Abba, Father.' So you are no longer a slave, but a son; and since you are a son, God has made you also an heir." He has promised to give us everything we need because we are His sons and daughters.

There's a kid living next door to us named Doug. He comes over a lot. Imagine him coming over one day and saying, "Hey, Barry, give me a quarter." What would I say?

Depending on what kind of mood I was in, I'd probably say, "Go home, beat it. Get a quarter from your mother. You're not *my* son."

But I have a son named Scott. He comes to me and says, "Dad, I want a dollar." And what do I say? "OK, Scott, here, take it." I do that because he's my boy.

God says we are His kids. He wants to treat us like sons and daughters. We are His heirs—the King's kids.

I don't give Scott everything he asks for. I know he doesn't need some of it. And I know some of it wouldn't be good for him. In the same way, God knows that some of the things we ask for aren't really needed or that they aren't good for us. And wisely, He withholds these things. But God the Father has given us everything we will ever need in Jesus Christ.

Several years ago I went home to visit my parents in West Virginia. My dad asked me to take a walk with him across the farm one afternoon. After a while we came to a beautiful tract of land. He turned to me and said, "Son, there is a piece of paper back at the house. It is the title to this piece of property. There are five acres here. I've put your name on the deed. It's yours now."

God has given us something far more precious than five acres of land. He put our names on the will of His Son, Jesus. When Jesus died, all that He had became ours. "Praise be to the God and Father of our Lord Jesus Christ, who has blessed us in heavenly realms with every spiritual blessing in Christ" (Ephesians 1:3). Peter wrote: "His divine power has given us everything we need for life and godliness" (2 Peter 1:3).

Why did He come? Jesus came in human form to identify with us. And He gave His life on the cross to redeem us, so that we might inherit all the blessings God has for us.

Sound good? It's better than that. But remember one thing—before the *crown* comes a *cross*. And that aspect of what Jesus did demands closer examination.

3

Bridging the Gap

The prisoner stood without speaking as the soldiers stripped him to the waist, tied his hands together, and bent his body across a rail. One of the soldiers picked up a whip made of leather strands into which bits of metal or bone had been tied at the ends. Then began the ordeal commonly called "the halfway death"—so called because it was intended to bring the victim just short of dying.

It was a form of torture peculiar to the Romans. The Jews did it differently. Their law limited flogging to a maximum of 39 strikes of the whip. But the Romans had no such rule. They flogged till the man doing the whipping got so tired he couldn't go on.

After the flogging, his back flayed open like a newly plowed field, the prisoner was led to the palace of the Roman governor. A company of soldiers, perhaps as many as 600, had gathered. They draped a purple robe, symbol of royalty, around the prisoner's shredded back so that the blood, as it coagulated, stuck to the fabric.

Someone had broken a branch from a thornbush and fastened the ends together to form a "crown." The soldiers placed it on the victim's head, jabbing the long thorns into his scalp. To complete the mockery, the soldiers struck his head with a rod, spit on him, and bowed down to him shouting, "Hail, king of the Jews!"

The prisoner reeled, half-conscious, before the jeering soldiers. A day of unimaginable punishment had just begun for the prisoner they called Jesus of Nazareth.

Place of the Skull

That same morning, a hideous procession wound its way through the crowded streets of Jerusalem. A heavy wooden beam had been lifted onto Jesus' bruised and bleeding shoulders. Weak from blood loss, pain, hunger, and lack of sleep, he stumbled forward. He carried on his back what was to form the horizontal beam of his cross.

Somewhere along the way, Jesus stumbled and fell. A man named Simon happened to be passing by, and the soldiers forced him to carry the cross beam.

When the procession reached Golgotha, a hill known as "the Place of the Skull," the soldiers nailed Jesus to a cross. They hammered a spike through each wrist, between the two long bones of the forearms. Next, they nailed his feet to the cross. Jesus' flesh ripped as the soldiers stood the cross upright and dropped its base into a hole in the ground.

By 3 o'clock that afternoon, Jesus' crucifixion,

an ordeal which the Roman historian Cicero called the most horrible torture ever devised by man, had ended. The man who claimed to be the Son of God was dead. And the question screaming in the minds of his followers was, "Why?" Why had it happened?

To understand the answer, we move ahead in time some 2,000 years to an isolated spot in the American Rockies. Five young men, ranging in age from 15 to 18, stand looking over a cliff.

They are backpackers. Nearing the end of a three-day hike, their path has been blocked by a chasm, some 100-feet deep and 20-feet wide. Since the five know of no other way to reach their destination, and since a dangerous storm is brewing in the mountains, they begin trying, one by one, to cross the chasm.

Making It on His Own

The first hiker to try crossing is Al Athlete. Al is tall, with muscles rippling all over his body. He's considered *the* big jock on campus. Nobody can match him in athletic skill or strength. Al has a philosophy about life. It goes something like this: "I'm a winner. I've got what it takes. I can do it because I try harder."

Al does 25 sit-ups and 25 push-ups to get warmed up for the jump. He puts on his $80 jumping shoes and starts his approach run.

By most standards, Al's jump would be impressive. He makes it about 28 feet—not far enough to get across. He crashes in a heap at the bottom of the chasm.

Faked Out by His Brain

If Al couldn't make it, perhaps another of the five hikers can—maybe Benny Bookworm. Benny is so clever in math that it doesn't take him long, with his pocket slide rule and his book of logarithmic tables, to figure out that the chasm is 30 feet, 3⁵⁄₁₆ inches across.

He also knows his exact body weight. So, according to the laws of velocity and momentum, Benny computes exactly how fast he needs to run, exactly what the wind resistance is, exactly how far and at what angle he has to jump to get across the chasm.

But something—perhaps only Benny could figure out exactly what—goes wrong. Despite his calculations, he only makes it 16 feet, 5⁶⁄₁₆ inches. Benny joins Al at the bottom of the chasm.

Where Money Fails

Milton Moneybags is next in line, and he looks a little ·worried. That's unusual. Milton has never had to worry. He's always had enough money to take care of most problems. All he's had to do is call Mom, and she'd come running with the car or the checkbook, or whatever else it was Milton needed.

Milton's money has opened a lot of doors for him, but when it comes to crossing the chasm, he does no better than his two friends. The best jumping equipment money could buy doesn't do the job. He ends up on the bottom with Al and Benny.

Popularity at Any Price

With their three fellow hikers lying lifelessly at the bottom of the cliff, you'd think the other two backpackers would take their chances with the storm. But not Conrad Clone, who's next in line. Conrad *always* follows the crowd. If the other guys smoke, so does Conrad. If they get drunk, he does too. If they fry their brains on dope, Conrad joins right in. If they go to church, he goes too.

The other guys had jumped. ... So, Conrad thinks over the situation—for about two seconds—then takes the plunge. So long, Conrad.

"Good Guys" Finish Last

The wind is really whipping down the mountainside now. The last hiker, Ronnie Religious, pulls his jacket around him as he considers his predicament. Ronnie has always had answers for everything—*pat* answers, perhaps, but answers. He proves almost every Sunday what a good guy he is. (The rest of the week doesn't count, in Ronnie's way of thinking.)

Ronnie's also active in his youth group. He's fairly certain that all his churchgoing will "pay off" when he takes his turn at the jump.

What Ronnie doesn't know is that he's no better off than Al Athlete, who trusted in his physical strength; or Benny Bookworm, who trusted in his brains; or Milton Moneybags, who trusted in his money. Being a "good guy" might impress a lot of people, but not 30-foot chasms. Ronnie joins his friends at the bottom.

The Wide Gap

So, what does this little make-believe tragedy have to do with why Jesus died? Let the mountainside chasm represent the gap that exists between God and man. Then let the efforts of Al, Benny, Milton, Conrad, and Ronnie stand for man's efforts to bridge the gap. And you begin to see the connection.

A tremendous gap stands between God and us, between His holiness and our selfishness. If we could see the holiness and absolute purity of God, we would understand how sinful we are and the difficulty involved in bridging the gap. We would understand why it's impossible for us to bridge the gap on our own.

In the Old Testament, Isaiah saw in a vision a glimpse of God sitting on His throne in heaven. Just a glimpse was all Isaiah needed to realize how sinful he was. "Woe to me," he cried, "I am ruined!" (Isaiah 6:5)

When Simon Peter realized that Jesus was God's Son, he said almost the same thing: "Go away from me, Lord; I am a sinful man!" (Luke 5:8)

What Peter had to learn is this: *God is holy, but He is also love.* He proved that love by Jesus' death on the cross. A 20-foot chasm is nothing compared to the wide gap which God's love and holiness had to span to reach sinful man.

Money can open fraternity and sorority doors. It can buy the "right" kinds of clothes. But it can't make anyone right with God. Ditto for physical strength, and brainpower—and even being a "good guy." People can't buy or earn what God alone is able to give.

Expensive Bridge-building

Peter wrote: "For Christ died for sins once for all, the righteous for the unrighteous, to bring you to God" (1 Peter 3:18). "He Himself bore our sins in His body on the tree, so that we might die to sins and live for righteousness" (1 Peter 2:24).

God bridged the gap. But at what a cost! Because salvation is free as far as man's part is concerned, we could get the impression that it didn't cost anything. But one look at Jesus on the cross shows what a tremendous price God paid.

Lots of people have pictures of the Crucifixion in their homes. But if someone painted a *realistic* picture of Jesus' death, it's doubtful that many people would put such a picture on their walls. It would be too gross to look at. And yet, the *spiritual* pain which Jesus experienced on the cross was even greater than His physical pain.

Why did He do it? Simple. He went through that pain so you and I wouldn't have to go through it. Two statements Jesus made while on the cross help explain this truth:

(1) "My God, My God, why have You forsaken Me?" (Matthew 27:46) As Jesus hung in agony on the cross, God the Father turned His back. For the first time ever, Jesus was totally separated from His Father's presence—flung to the other side of the chasm, going through hell so you and I wouldn't have to.

At this point Jesus took on Himself all of the garbage from our lives. He took our sin on Himself, the Bible says (1 Peter 2:24). As a result, His fellowship with God the Father was broken. Think about the sinful things you've done. And realize that God's Son was forsaken by His Father in order to take care of *your* sin problem. Unbelievable!

It's impossible for us to fully understand how much it cost Jesus to bridge the gap. But understand this: He did it for you.

(2) "It is finished" (John 19:30). This final statement of Jesus on the cross was not a confession of defeat, but of victory. The chasm had been bridged! Jesus had paid the full price for mankind's forgiveness. Because of that payment, you and I can be totally forgiven and accepted by God. "If we confess our sins, He is faithful and just to forgive us our sins and to cleanse us from all unrighteousness" (1 John 1:9, KJV).

Not only did Jesus' death provide forgiveness, it also provided freedom from *guilt*: "There is therefore now no condemnation for those who are in Christ Jesus" (Romans 8:1, NASB).

Not only was sin forgiven and guilt taken away, but the curse of *death* was broken. The story doesn't end with Jesus' death. Three days later He burst out of the grave.

I learned a dramatic lesson in the meaning of Jesus' resurrection when a high school friend was dying of cancer. This friend, with whom I had run track had shriveled to 96 pounds. I visited him in the hospital and then talked with his mother.

"Barry," she asked me, "where is God?" At that moment, I had no answer. Then I realized, *He's in the same place He was 2,000 years ago when His own Son was dying.* For the first time, I really understood that in Jesus Christ the sting of death is removed. Jesus finished off death!

In the movie, *The Greatest Story Ever Told*, the camera focuses on the cross, then on Jesus' feet. Blood and rain drip down His legs and fall into a puddle below the cross. The puddle turns red. Then it overflows and runs down the hill. The hill slowly turns red. Finally, the blood flows into a river which turns red, then into the ocean—it too turns red. The scene symbolizes the fact that Jesus died for the whole world.

He died for His critics and enemies who stood gloating that day because they'd managed to see Him killed. He died for the bystanders who really didn't care about Him one way or the other. He died for the small group of His followers who stood beneath the cross watching Him die. And He died for you and me.

4

The Resurrection—
Rip-off or Reality?

Anyone can kill another person. But what about bringing someone back to life? The Russians have weapons equal to 35 tons of TNT for every person in the world. But that's Mickey Mouse stuff compared to the power it would take to bring someone back from the dead.

Jesus claimed access to that kind of power. He told His disciples, "Listen, we are going down to Jerusalem. I will suffer and die there, but keep cool because three days later I will rise again" (Matthew 16:21-26; Mark 8:31-38; 9:9; Luke 9:18-25, *author's paraphrase*). He made it plain that everything He said and did would hinge on the Resurrection.

So, whether or not Jesus was raised from the dead is extremely significant. The Apostle Paul said, "If Christ has not been raised, our preaching is useless and so is your faith" (1 Corinthians 15:14).

Jesus' resurrection is important because it establishes His *uniqueness*. No other religious leader has ever claimed to be raised from the dead. If we could visit the graves of Buddha, Mohammed, Confucius, or numerous others who started religious movements, we would find dead bodies. But at the tomb of Jesus all we find is an empty grave.

Whether or not Jesus was raised from the dead is also important because if it is *not* true, then we have been ripped off. Christianity and the church is one big lie, and we are wasting our time being involved with it.

Jesus' resurrection is important for another reason: If it *is* true, then Jesus Christ has the right and the power to change your life. Jesus said, "I am the resurrection and the life. He who believes in Me will live, even though he dies, and whoever lives and believes in Me will never die" (John 11:25-26).

Did Jesus Christ really rise from the dead? The evidence says yes! That doesn't mean that the validity of Christianity can be "proven" like the latest scientific theory. God, as the saying goes, will not be crammed into test tubes. But faith in Jesus Christ, and in the reality of His resurrection, does not have to be "blind" faith. The historical evidence stacks up solidly on the side of the Christian belief—that Jesus was raised from the dead.

The Witness of the Scholars

Some people believe that all educated persons consider the Resurrection a myth. The fact is that many great thinkers have defended the truth of Jesus' being raised from the dead. In fact, for 429 years after Jesus lived, no one wrote a single word disputing the reality of the Resurrection.[1]

Professor Thomas Arnold, chairman of Modern History at Oxford University, said: "I have been used for many years to study the histories of other times, and to examine and weigh the evidence of those who have written about them, and I know of no one fact in the history of mankind which is proved by better and fuller evidence of every sort, to the understanding of a fair inquirer, than the great sign which God has given us that Christ died and rose again from the dead."[2]

Lord Lyndhurst, one of the greatest legal authorities in English history wrote, "I know pretty well what evidence is; and I tell you such evidence as that for the Resurrection has never broken down yet."[3]

Simon Greenleaf, who died in 1853, was a great professor of law at Harvard. His books are still studied in law schools today. Two students challenged Greenleaf concerning whether or not the Resurrection would stand in a court of law. He took the challenge. His conclusion was that the Resurrection would stand in any court of law. He said, "the resurrection of Jesus Christ is the most established fact of history."[4]

Frank Morison, lawyer, engineer, rationalist, thought Jesus' life had been a good example for the world, but he could not buy the "resurrection myth." He set out to disprove it, and finished his research a believer.[5]

Lord Lyttleton and Gilbert Benjamin West were professors at Oxford University. They took a six-month study leave and set out to disprove the resurrection of Jesus Christ and the conversion of Paul. Concluding their research, they both admitted that the Resurrection and Paul's conversion could be substantiated from a scholar's standpoint. They then gave their lives to Jesus Christ.

On the flyleaf of the book they co-authored as a result of their study, they wrote: "Blame not before thou hast examined the truth." In other words, don't reject till you have examined the evidence.[6]

Josh McDowell, speaker and author, faced up to the Resurrection issue during his college days. Several of his Christian friends challenged McDowell, who was not a Christian, to intellectually examine the claims of Christ. After studying the evidence, he came to the conclusion that he would have been "intellectually dishonest" with himself if he did not believe. He now travels to college campuses worldwide sharing his insights on the validity of Jesus Christ as the Son of God.[7]

McDowell has this to say on the Resurrection: "A believer in Jesus Christ today can have complete confidence, as did the first Christians, that his faith is based not on myth or legend, but on the solid historical fact of the risen Christ and the empty tomb."[8]

From a historical viewpoint, educators, lawyers, and scientists alike have confirmed the validity of the Resurrection. The witness of the scholars indicates that *Jesus is alive*.

Now let's look at some of the facts of the actual resurrection event.

The Undisturbed Grave Clothes

"Early on the first day of the week, while it was still dark, Mary of Magdala went to the tomb and saw that the stone had been removed from the entrance. So she came running to Simon Peter and the other disciple, the one Jesus loved, and said, 'They have taken the Lord out of the tomb, and we don't know where they have put him!'

"So Peter and the other disciple started for the tomb. Both were running, but the other disciple outran Peter and reached the tomb first. He bent over and looked in at the strips of linen lying there but did not go in. Then Simon Peter, who was behind him, arrived and went into the tomb. He saw the strips of linen lying there, as well as the burial cloth that had been around Jesus' head. The cloth was folded up by itself, separate from the linen. Finally the other disciple, who had reached the tomb first, also went inside. He saw and believed" (John 20:1-8).

Here, we see Mary Magdalene coming to the grave of Jesus. When she saw that the stone had been rolled back, she ran away. She wanted to believe, but she was afraid. She was like many students are the day the teacher hands back the final exam grades. They are so nervous that not only do they eat their erasers but they are too psyched out to even look at their grades.

That's the way Mary was. She wanted to look inside the tomb, but she was afraid. So she ran to Peter and John and told them that the stone had been moved.

Then Peter and John headed for the tomb. John, a member of the Jerusalem High track team sprinted ahead. Peter, a tackle at Galilee High, plodded along behind. John got to the tomb first, then came to a screeching halt. Why? Suddenly, he realized . . . it was dark . . . he was in a graveyard . . . and a body was missing! John waited for Peter, then let the big man lead the way.

What did they see? Whatever it was must have been significant because these few Bible verses mention three times that Peter and John "saw." The word used for "saw" means "to see and understand." They saw the wrapping with no body in it. They saw the burial cloth that had been wound around Jesus' head "folded up by itself" (John 20:7). With this evidence in front of them, they "saw and believed."

The Empty Tomb

Matthew 27:57-66 records the many precautions that were taken in the burial of Jesus' body. The Jewish authorities were afraid Jesus' disciples would steal the body, then claim that He was alive. They took several steps which, along with some of the normal burial procedures, would make sure that Jesus stayed in the tomb. Or so they thought.

First, they put Him in a "new tomb" (v. 60) carved out of solid rock. Inside, were several stone slabs recessed into the walls of the cave. Eventually a body was to be placed on each slab.

Second, Jesus' body was wrapped in a "clean linen cloth" (v. 59). The body was brought in and laid on one of the stone slabs. According to the Jewish burial custom, the people who buried Jesus also brought about 75 pounds of spices—myrrh and aloes (John 19:39-40).

With yards of linen cloth, they wrapped the body, placing the spices and a gummy substance on the wrapping. They wrapped the cloth around the legs, then around the trunk up to the neck. Then the spices and gummy substance hardened. Jesus probably weighed about 100 pounds more than His normal body weight. He was a mummy! Imagine how hard it would have been to get out of those wrappings.

Third, a "big stone" was rolled against the door. We don't know just how much the stone weighed, though some authorities speculate it was as much as two tons. Almost all agree it would have taken at least three or four men to move it, once the stone was placed in the tomb entrance.

Not only was the stone heavy, but the tomb entrance was on a downward slope. The stone was perched above it. In closing the tomb, the big stone was let loose and it crashed into the rut in front of the tomb opening. So, gravity would have made the stone even more difficult to move.

Fourth, the tomb was made "secure by sealing the stone" (Matthew 27:66). Cords were stretched and fastened across the stone. The Roman emperor's official insignia was inscribed in clay or wax on the outside of the tomb. If anyone broke the seal, it meant death. Jesus wasn't supposed to get out!

Fifth, the Romans placed a "guard" (v. 65) around the tomb. Josh McDowell observes that many people picture the "guard" as two skinny guys holding wooden spears and wearing mini-skirts. But the real picture is of a 16-man security unit with each man responsible for 6 square feet of territory! These were Roman soldiers—the best in the world. Their methods are still used by military men today.

So what happened? There are a bunch of theories. Let's examine them.

One view is that *the Roman and Jewish leaders took the body*. But these leaders were the ones who had just put Jesus' body in there. Why would they want it out? They wouldn't. They wanted to protect their careers and they knew that if Jesus' body were missing, all of Palestine would be in an uproar. They wanted to keep the body in the tomb.

In addition, they certainly would have come up with the body after the disciples started preaching that Jesus was alive. The disciples were preaching only a few minutes away from the tomb. The whole city was stirred up about Jesus. In an effort to destroy Christianity, these Roman and Jewish leaders beat the disciples, jailed them, and told them not to preach. All the authorities had to do was to produce the body and the uproar would have been over. But they couldn't produce it because they didn't have it.

A second view is that *the disciples stole the body*. That's what the Roman and Jewish authorities wanted people to think, according to Matthew 28:11-15. But remember the guards—the 16 soldiers who were among the best in the world? If the guards allowed the emperor's seal to be broken, they would be brutally punished.

One form of punishment that might have been used called for a soldier's clothes to be taken off and placed at his feet. Then he was burned to death, his own clothes being used for fuel. No way were the guards going to let Jesus' body get away!

Now, remember the disciples? Eleven scruffy guys coming to take on the best soldiers in the world. You've got to be kidding! They couldn't even "toilet paper" someone's house without getting caught. The match-up would be like a 7th-grade football team taking on the Dallas Cowboys.

Imagine the disciples sneaking up on the guards. They steal the soldiers' swords and wipe them out. They push away the huge stone. They steal the body and tell everybody that Jesus is alive. It takes super blind faith to believe that!

The disciples could not have taken the body. First, they could never have overcome the Romans. Second, when persecuted and facing death for their faith in Christ, surely one of them would have admitted that the Resurrection was a lie. Not one of them ever did.

A third explanation of the Resurrection is *the "Swoon Theory."* Hugh Schoenfeld in his book *The Passover Plot* theorizes that Jesus never died on the cross. He was merely thought to be dead. He was taken down from the cross and put into the tomb. The coolness of the tomb revived Him. He got out and showed Himself to His disciples, and claimed to be risen from the dead.

Imagine it! Jesus went through all of the suffering described in the last chapter. Blood mixed with water poured out of His side, providing medical evidence of His death. Several people handled His body and raised no questions about it being alive. Jesus was wrapped in mummifying substances and put in a cold, dark tomb with no food or water.

So He revives, gets out of His mummy case, pushes away the huge stone, overcomes 16 of the world's best soldiers, walks to Jerusalem on nail-pierced feet, and appears to His disciples as the picture of health. No way, Jose!

The best explanation is the biblical one: the

tomb was empty because Jesus Christ was raised from the dead!

The Ten Appearances

The Bible tells us that Jesus appeared 10 different times in 40 days after His resurrection. He was seen by as many as 500 people and by as few as 1. He cooked. He ate fish. He talked. Some of His disciples even touched Him.

Could all of these people who said they saw Him have had hallucinations? For that many people on that many occasions to have had hallucinations would break all the laws of psychology. No. *Jesus is alive!*

The Disciples' Changed Lives

One of the greatest evidences for the Resurrection is the *changed lives* of Jesus' disciples. When Jesus was arrested, Peter let a young servant girl scare him into denying Christ (John 18:15-18). After Jesus died, Peter and the other disciples hid out, afraid for their lives (John 20:19). But after witnessing Jesus' resurrection, the disciples appeared before the same court that only a few weeks before had condemned Jesus to death.

Peter courageously challenged the court: "It [the healing of a crippled man] is by the name of Jesus Christ of Nazareth, whom you crucified but whom God raised from the dead, that this man [the cripple] stands before you completely healed. . . . Salvation is found in no one else for there is no other name under heaven given to men by which we must be saved" (Acts 4:10,12).

The court realized that Peter and John had been changed. "When they saw the courage of Peter and John and realized that they were unschooled, ordinary men, they were astonished and they took note that these men had been with Jesus" (Acts 4:13).

James, the brother of Jesus, had thought all along that Jesus was one brick shy of a full load. (See Mark 3:20-21.) If your brother went around saying, "I am the Door," "I am the Water," "I am the Good Shepherd," "I am God," you would think he was weird too!

Then, convinced of the reality of the Resurrection, James recognized Jesus for who He really is. Listen to how he begins his book: "James, a servant of God and of the Lord Jesus Christ" (James 1:1).

Mark, who wrote the second Gospel, was a young boy when Jesus taught the crowds in Galilee. Changed by the power of the Resurrection, Mark became a man. When asked to choose between denying Jesus' resurrection or dying, he chose death.

According to tradition, his killers tied a rope to each limb of his body, then tied a horse to each rope. Then they pulled his body apart. Mark knew the truth about the Resurrection and he was willing to die for it.

Then there is Paul—how do we explain him? His passion in life was to persecute Christians. Changed by resurrection power, he proclaimed Jesus throughout the world. His number one goal in life was "to know Him and the power of His resurrection, and that I may share His sufferings, becoming like Him in His death" (Philippians 3:10).

All of Jesus' disciples, except John, were killed for their faith in Jesus. People will lie to protect themselves. But people don't die for something they know to be a lie!

Personal Evidence

The miracle of changed lives is one piece of evidence that can be observed firsthand today. Hardened criminals become model citizens. Atheists become dedicated believers. Drug addicts are set free—and give Jesus the credit.

The changes in my own life have been less dramatic. But they are nonetheless a testimony to the power of the resurrected Jesus.

In my teen years, I was selfish, cocky, overly ambitious, hungry for popularity, and insensitive to people. Then the resurrection power of Jesus changed my life. Some of the most significant changes came in my family relationships.

One afternoon, when I was 16 and my sister Cathey was 13, I was working on a science poster. Cathey brought me something to drink and when she offered me the glass, I ignored her. She stood there for a moment and when I still didn't take the glass, she poured it all over my poster. I jumped up and slapped her. She ran into the house and I ran after her. I was going to hit her again.

From that point on, our relationship drifted farther and farther apart. Even when I tried to do something nice for Cathey, it never seemed to work out. Later, Cathey began to have some personal difficulties. In the middle of that period she told my mom, "You know, Barry has really been a crummy big brother to me." My mom told me what Cathey had said, and it broke my heart.

You see, since the science poster episode, I had received Jesus into my life, and my life had changed. I asked Him to show me how to have a good relationship with my sister.

One day I talked with her and confessed, "Cathey, I *have* been a crummy big brother to you." I listed all of the ways I had failed her. Then I asked, "Cathey, will you forgive me?" With tears in her eyes, she slid across the couch, put her arms around me and said, "Barry, I love you and I forgive you." Immediately the barriers were gone—smashed by the resurrection power of Jesus Christ!

A Decision That Makes Sense

The resurrection of Jesus Christ is no rip-off. It's reality. So many people reject the truth without examining the evidence. Add to the evidence for the Resurrection hundreds of fulfilled Bible prophecies, the impact of Jesus' life and teachings, and His work in the world today—and believing in Jesus makes good sense.

But mentally accepting the evidence is not enough. Jesus is alive. But are you willing to let Him live in you? When you allow His resurrection power to control you, several things happen:

(1) *You have the life of Jesus in you.* "You, however, are controlled not by the sinful nature but by the Spirit, if the Spirit of God lives in you. And

if anyone does not have the Spirit of Christ, he does not belong to Christ. But if Christ is in you, your body is dead because of sin, yet your spirit is alive because of righteousness. And if the spirit of Him who raised Jesus from the dead is living in you, He who raised Christ from the dead will also give life to your mortal bodies through His Spirit who lives in you" (Romans 8:9-11).

(2) You are made new. "Therefore, if anyone is in Christ, he is a new creation; the old has gone, the new has come!" (2 Corinthians 5:17)

(3) You have all you need to live life at its best. "Praise be to the God and Father of our Lord Jesus Christ, who has blessed us in the heavenly realms with every spiritual blessing in Christ" (Ephesians 1:3).

(4) You no longer have to fear death. "Where, O death, is your victory? Where, O death, is your sting? The sting of death is sin, and the power of sin is the Law. But thanks be to God! He gives us the victory through our Lord Jesus Christ" (1 Corinthians 15:55-57).

(5) You will live with God forever. "I write these things to you who believe in the name of the Son of God, so that you may know that you have eternal life" (1 John 5:13).

If you have asked Jesus into your life, you already have access to His resurrection power. Pray for that power to control you every day.

If you have not asked Jesus into your life, you can do that now by sincerely praying a simple prayer, such as the following:

Lord Jesus, I want to know You and Your resurrection power. I admit to You that I am a sinner. I ask You now to forgive my sins. And I invite

You to come into my life, to live in me and control me. By faith I thank You for coming into my life this moment.

Amen.

---

[1]Paul L. Maier, "The Empty Tomb Is History," *Christianity Today*, vol. XIX, 13, March 28, 1975, p. 6.

[2]Thomas Arnold, *Christian Life—Its Hopes, Its Fears and Its Close* (London: T. Fellowes, 1859, 6th ed.), p. 324.

[3]Wilbur M. Smith, *Therefore Stand: Christian Apologetics* (cited by Josh McDowell, *Evidence That Demands a Verdict* (San Bernardino, Campus Crusade for Christ, 1972), p. 198.

[4]Simon Greenleaf, *Testimony of the Evangelists, Examined by the Rules of Evidence Administered in Courts of Justice* (Grand Rapids: Baker Book House, 1965, reprinted from 1847 ed.), pp. 28-30.

[5]Frank Morison, *Who Moved the Stone?* (London: Faber and Faber, 1930).

[6]Michael Green, *Man Alive* (Downers Grove, Inter-Varsity Press, 1968), pp. 55-56.

[7]Josh McDowell, *Evidence That Demands a Verdict* (San Bernardino, Campus Crusade for Christ, 1971), p. 373.

[8]Josh McDowell, *More Than a Carpenter* (Wheaton: Tyndale House Publishers, Inc.), p. 98.

5

Knowing Jesus

If being cocky and self-sufficient when I was in high school wasn't bad enough, I also used people to accomplish my goals. That arrogant, know-it-all person was one side of me—the real side. The other side of me was the nice guy, who was friendly to everybody and who went to church every Sunday. I was a leader in the church youth group. I knew a lot about the Bible. And I could act religious when the situation called for it.

I was like the little boy who came running into his house one day yelling, "Mommy, Mommy, look!" He was carrying a dead mouse with him, dangling it by the tail.

"I killed him, Mommy," he blurted. "I ran over him with my bike, then I hit him with my baseball bat, and my soccer shoe, and my football—" About that time, the boy realized that the preacher had come to visit. Suddenly an angelic look came across the boy's face as he finished his sentence ". . . and the little mouse went home to be with the Lord."

That's the way I lived my life. I could be religious when I was in church on Sundays. But Mondays through Saturdays, Christianity had little effect on the way I lived my life.

A lot of people live that way. It's easy for them to act like Christians in church. But the rest of the time, their lives demonstrate that they don't really know Jesus Christ in a personal way.

The Apostle Paul *knew* Jesus! In his letter to the Philippians, Paul described the change that had taken place in his life. He said, "All these things that I once thought very worthwhile—now I've thrown them all away so that I can put my trust and hope in Christ alone. Yes, everything is worthless when compared with the priceless gain of knowing Christ Jesus my Lord" (Philippians 3:7-8, LB).

For Paul, knowing the *facts* about Jesus Christ wasn't good enough. He wanted a dynamic, personal relationship with Jesus. It's having that kind of relationship that makes Christianity come alive.

When you date someone, you can learn all kinds of facts about that person. But if it's someone you care for, having the facts is nothing compared to going out with that person. You enjoy being with someone you care for. When you receive Jesus Christ into your life, you begin a relationship with Him. Though it's important to know the facts about Jesus, what's most important is knowing and loving Him more and more as your relationship grows.

Paul was determined to have that kind of relationship with Jesus. So he set some goals. They're found in Philippians 3:10. Paul wanted (1) to know Christ, (2) to know the power of His resurrection, (3) to know the fellowship of sharing in His sufferings, and (4) to become like Him.

Getting Personal

"I want to know Christ . . ."

Soon after I got to college, I discovered that I was no longer the terrific success I had been in high school. Since first grade, I had always played a lot of basketball. It was a major part of my life. But when I got to Davidson College, I discovered that my scrawny six-foot body looked like a midget's beside the 6' 6", 6' 8", and 6' 10" guys on the team.

I tried hard. I continued to shoot, even though my giant teammates kept smashing the ball back into my face. I kept playing defense, even though my body got plastered to the court on a regular basis. Finally I began to suspect that the goal I had set of making all-conference wasn't very realistic.

I've already mentioned what my social life was like during my freshman year—a total disaster— as illustrated by the blind date my second week at school.

I had also set some academic goals. I had decided I was going to be at least a B student. Then my first test came—in history, the subject in which I had planned to major. I studied like crazy. But when the test results came back, I found out I had made a 74, a D. I had never made a D in my life.

Being the self-sufficient person that I was, I decided I would just have to study harder. I spent as much time as I possibly could preparing for the next test. And I didn't get a 74 on that one; I got a 47! My academic goals were slipping down the tube fast. It was as if all the props I had depended on were being knocked out from under me.

I remember homecoming weekend. I was lonely, homesick, and depressed. Saturday morning I stared out my dorm window and asked myself, *Who am I? What am I doing here? Where am I going?*—questions I'd never seriously considered. One thing I finally realized—I wasn't sufficient in myself.

I began to search for answers beyond myself. In the following months, I looked for answers in intellectualism, in philosophy, in social relationships, in athletics. The more I searched, the emptier I felt. I finished my freshman year feeling that the entire year had been a waste.

That summer I attended a camp in the mountains of North Carolina. My first day there I met a beautiful girl and decided I wanted to ask her out. I asked her to go to church with me that night, and she agreed.

After church, we took a walk down a lonely, dark road. We talked for a while, then I started to ease my arm around her to kiss her.

"No," she said firmly.

No girl had ever done that to me. In the frustration of the moment, I did something dumb. I asked her, "Why not?"

"Because of Jesus Christ," she replied.

I remember standing there in the dark, scratching my head and thinking, *What does Jesus Christ have to do with kissing?* Only later did I understand that a relationship with Jesus affects every area of a person's life.

But this girl intrigued me. I saw that there was something different about her, a quality of life that I hadn't seen in other girls I had dated. Somehow I understood that she knew Jesus Christ in a way

I had never known Him.

At the same camp, I met a basketball player from the University of Tennessee. I enjoyed playing ball with him. I soon realized that he had that same quality of life I was seeing in my girl friend. The two of them influenced me to think seriously about my relationship with Jesus Christ. My search had taken a significant turn.

I began to realize several truths:

- God loves me.
- God loves me more than I love myself (and that was a lot!)
- God loves me as much now as He would if I were the only person in the world.
- God proved His love for me. "But God demonstrates His own love for us in this: While we were still sinners, Christ died for us" (Romans 5:8).

My search led me to the Bible, and I began to grasp the truth of verses like this one: "God showed how much He loved us by sending His only Son into this wicked world to bring us eternal life through His death. In this act we see what real love is: it is not our love for God, but His love for us when He sent His Son to satisfy God's anger against our sins" (1 John 4:9-10, LB).

The influence of my two new friends, my own searching, and the unseen working of the Holy Spirit, led me to a decision. One night I knelt beside a chair and said, "Jesus, I've called myself a Christian for a long time, but I need You to become real to me. I want You to come into my life the way You've come into the lives of my two friends. I want You to make me what You want me to be."

And Jesus did come into my life! There was no thunder or lightning, no trumpets, no angels—only a calm peace that came over me. It wasn't an emotional experience, but it was real. That was the beginning point for me of getting to know Jesus.

Living in Overdrive

"I want to know ... the power of His resurrection ..."

One day, about a year and a half after my experience of receiving Christ, I was sitting in my room at Davidson College. The thought came to me, *Barry, maybe you shouldn't be playing basketball.* My next thought went something like this: *St. Clair, that's about the dumbest idea you've ever had.*

I had been playing basketball from the time I was in first grade. And since fourth grade I'd been playing on organized teams. In the winter I would sweep the snow off the outside court and play basketball with my gloves on. During the summer before my senior year in high school, I practiced eight hours a day every day so I could play up to my maximum potential the next season.

Everything in my life revolved around the game. I wanted nothing more than to play college basketball and, perhaps, to make all-conference. Quitting was out of the question. So I pushed the thought out of my mind.

But the thought kept coming back—*Maybe you shouldn't be playing basketball.* One day I was reading the Bible and came across Matthew 6:33:

"But seek first His kingdom and His righteousness, and all these things will be given to you as
well."

"Seek first what God wants," the verse seemed
to say to me. And I had to admit, *Barry, you've
been playing basketball all this time. You've been
a Christian for a year and a half. But you've never
offered to give basketball up to God—never.*

God seemed to be asking, "Are you serious about
Me?" I knew He wanted me to give up the most
important thing in my life. Or at least to be willing
to give it up. But I wasn't sure I was willing. Just
the thought of giving up basketball made me sick.

For several weeks I struggled with the issue.
One Saturday my parents came to visit me, and I
told them about my struggle. Sitting in the Davidson College parking lot, we talked, and cried,
and prayed.

Finally I decided I would give up basketball—
scholarship and all. It was serious business, but
I believed God wanted me to do it.

That experience was a significant turning point
for me. It was at that point that I began to discover
the *resurrection power* of Jesus Christ in my life.
I began to grow spiritually—and to know Jesus—
much more than ever before. The key to the new
power I was experiencing was one simple word:
obedience. God wanted me to obey Him and when
I did, I began to experience the kind of power in
my life that He wanted me to have.

God wants every Christian to experience this
power in his life—the *same power* that raised Jesus
from the dead! Jesus wants to change us. And He
changes us through His resurrection power working in us.

Paul wrote: "I pray that you will begin to understand how incredibly great His power is to help those who believe Him. It is that same mighty power that raised Christ from the dead and seated Him in the place of honor at God's right hand in heaven" (Ephesians 1:20).

That power is in every Christian, because Jesus is in every Christian. That resurrection power works in us as we *obey* Jesus Christ. "Whoever has My commands and obeys them, he is the one who loves Me. He who loves Me will be loved by My Father, and I too will love him and show Myself to him" (John 14:21).

The fact that I quit basketball does not mean that's what God wants everyone to do! What He really wants is our hearts. For me, obedience to Jesus meant giving up the hours I spent eating and sleeping basketball. For someone else, it may mean making a relationship right with parents. It may involve a boyfriend or girlfriend . . . or popularity . . . or some habit. . . . But till we are willing to obey Jesus completely, we won't really know Him or the power of His resurrection.

My basketball story has a significant footnote: Two years after I gave up basketball, the Lord gave it back to me. I had the opportunity to travel with Athletes in Action, an all-Christian team that competes against major colleges and universities. It uses basketball to gain a hearing for the Gospel of Jesus Christ.

In one summer I traveled to 5 countries—Japan, Korea, Taiwan, Hong Kong, and the Philippines—playing 50 games in 7 weeks. At every game, my teammates and I had the opportunity to tell fans and players about Jesus Christ.

Once I gave basketball over to God, He gave it back to me—to use for His glory. That's resurrection power at work!

Paying the Price

"I want to know . . . the fellowship of sharing in His sufferings . . ."

Another of the Apostle Paul's goals was to know "the fellowship of sharing in His sufferings." Some people have the idea that becoming a Christian makes all of life's problems disappear. Baloney!

God never promised that the Christian life would be a made-in-the-shade way of living. In fact what He did promise was just the opposite of the easy life. "For it has been granted to you on behalf of Christ not only to believe on Him, but also to suffer for Him" (Philippians 1:29).

Many people discover that they have more problems after they receive Christ than before. That's because becoming a Christian brings them into conflict with the world. Christians often take life more seriously. They get involved in sticky situations like speaking out against injustice and standing up for truth when the truth's not popular. But on the positive side, these pressures push Christians closer to Jesus and cause them to grow stronger in Him. Christians may have more problems, but they also have the Problem Solver to help them.

Several years ago my wife Carol and I were at a conference center near Asheville, North Carolina. We had been having a wonderful time on the beautiful grounds. But I had a nagging, frustrated feeling that I couldn't shake. God seemed light years away from me. For several months before the conference, I had had this miserable feeling, and it all came to a head during the conference.

The Lord brought to mind a certain sin in my past that I have never confessed to Him or tried to make right. I had thought about the incident before, but I had never admitted to myself that it was a problem. I hadn't even been able to tell Carol about it. This time I realized that the problem had to be taken care of.

First I confessed the sin to the Lord. I knew He forgave me, but further action needed to be taken. I told Carol what had been bothering me. "When I was in college I cheated on some German tests. Deep down inside, for a long time, I've known something's been wrong. Now I know that if I'm going to be the person God wants me to be, I need to get this problem straightened out."

When Carol and I returned home, I phoned the German professor. Talking to him was the last thing in the world I wanted to do. But I knew it was right. "Doc," I said, "I cheated on some of your tests. That was wrong. Will you forgive me?"

He said, "Sure, Barry, I forgive you."

It was one of the hardest things I've ever done in my life. But I can't express the feeling I had when I finished apologizing to the professor and hung up the phone. I felt as if a weight had been lifted. I almost floated out of the room. I was *free!*

Through this experience I began to understand what the "fellowship of His suffering" is all about. Doing the right thing—what Christ wants—sometimes means Christians have to pay a price, to suffer.

When we are willing to suffer, to face up to the hard things and meet them head-on, God can deal with the problems in such a way that He sets us totally free from them. "If the Son sets you free, you will be free indeed" (John 8:36).

So many believers never get free from the things that keep them bound up. They stay in their miserable conditions because they aren't willing to pay the price required to straighten out their problems and be free. They're not willing to go through the Cross—the suffering—in order to get to the Resurrection—the power that sets people free.

But as Christians we have the privilege of identifying ourselves with the cross of Christ, as Paul did. He wrote: "I have been crucified with Christ and I no longer live, but Christ lives in me. The life I live in the body, I live by faith in the Son of God, who loved me and gave Himself for me" (Galatians 2:20).

Identifying with the Cross means more than wearing one on a chain around our necks. It means facing up daily to the problems that face us. It means dealing with problems and sins the way Jesus wants us to deal with them—no matter how much it may hurt.

You never experience the Resurrection till you go through the Cross. You never experience the power till you go through the suffering.

Changing

"Becoming like Him . . ."

In stating his fourth goal, Paul said, I want to become "like Him [Christ] in His death" (Philip-

pians 3:10). Some people believe that Paul was
referring to the spiritual process of dying to *self*,
so that Christ's resurrection power could work in
him. Others believe that Paul wanted so much to
be like Jesus that He could consider it an honor
to die physically in the same way Jesus died. Either
way, it's obvious that one of Paul's main goals was
to be like Jesus.

Someone asked a famous sculptor to explain how
he had made a statue of a horse. The sculptor answered, "You just take a piece of granite and chip
away everything that isn't horse."

As we get to know Jesus, and experience the
power of His resurrection and the fellowship of
His sufferings, God begins shaping us to be like
Jesus. He begins to chip away at certain areas of
our lives that prevent us from being like Jesus.
And sometimes it's painful. But the areas that God
takes away are those that keep us from reaching
the goal He has in mind for us.

God has a unique plan, a blueprint, for our lives.
He wants to make us like His Son. "For from the
very beginning God decided that those who came
to Him—and all along He knew who would—
should become like His Son" (Romans 8:29, LB).

Some people think that if we allow God to make
us like His Son we will lose our individuality, our
uniqueness. But that isn't true. We will always be
uniquely ourselves. Changed, yes. Better, yes. But
still unique.

Some children don't look much like their brothers and sisters. But even though they don't look
like each other, in some way each one resembles
his father or mother. One might have his father's
nose, another might have her mother's eye color

and hair color, another his father's height or some other distinctive feature. The kids don't look like each other, but they all look something like their parents.

That's how it is in God's family. God doesn't destroy our individual identities, but He changes us so that we all resemble Jesus. God is at work in us day by day to make us like His Son.

Paul wanted to know Jesus. He wanted to know the power of His resurrection and the fellowship of His suffering, and to be like Him. Jesus wants every Christian to know Him that way.

6

Jesus Is Lord!

Your best friend is coming to your home for the first time. And you really would like for it to look decent. Everything looks OK as the two of you walk into the living room. But then the embarrassment begins. . . .

You enter the kitchen. All the pots and pans from dinner are in the sink. And your little brother has left a banana peel hanging halfway out of the garbage can. It's overflowing and should have been emptied, but you forgot.

In the bathroom, someone didn't clean the sink after shaving—and your little brother has done it again. . . . The kid's been trying for years to learn how to brush his teeth. But the junk splattered all over the mirror indicates he still hasn't mastered the technique.

In addition, your sister's soggy, false eyelashes are lying on the sink. You wish you could duck into the woodwork somewhere instead of standing around looking dumb.

Now your guest is headed for your bedroom,

which should have been cordoned off as a disaster area. Clothes lie in piles on the floor. Old posters, hanging by a single piece of tape, curl outward from the wall. Your mother has kept the vow she made six months ago when she promised not to make up your bed again. Consequently your white sheets are now a lovely brown.

Letting in a Friend

Did you ever realize how much our lives are like a house? Some of us lock Jesus out of our lives because we are afraid He wouldn't like what He would find inside. Others of us let Him in, then we keep Him out of certain rooms where we keep all of the junk. We don't realize that Jesus already knows everything about us, even the things hidden deep in the back corners of our lives. He knows what's inside us.

Even when He was on earth in a human body, Jesus could tell what was happening inside people. John wrote: "But Jesus did not commit Himself unto them, because He knew all men, and needed not that any should testify of man: for He knew what was in man" (John 2:24-25, KJV).

Jesus knows what is in us. Nothing is hidden from Him. He won't enter any room into which He isn't invited, but He knows what is there anyway.

The reason He wants to enter our lives is not to embarrass us. He wants to do something about the mess that causes us embarrassment. He would like permission to come in and haul out all the garbage and clean up the house.

Gentleman, Lord

Right this minute Jesus Christ is Lord—absolute master and ruler—of the entire universe! The day will come when every person in the world will acknowledge that fact. "Therefore God exalted Him to the highest place and gave Him the name that is above every name, that at the name of Jesus every knee should bow, in heaven and on earth and under the earth, and every tongue confess that Jesus Christ is Lord, to the glory of God the Father" (Philippians 2:9-11).

Since Jesus is Lord, He has the right to everything in His creation, including our lives. He created us, and He payed for us with His own blood. So we belong to Him. "You are not your own; you were bought at a price" (1 Corinthians 6:19-20).

Jesus has a right to come into any area of our lives that He chooses. But He is a gentleman. He doesn't enter without knocking first, and He won't come into any room that we don't ask Him to enter.

One way we avoid letting Jesus into parts of our lives is by trying to clean them up ourselves. We try hard to break bad habits. We try to clean up our language and our lustful thoughts and actions. We try to get along with our parents and brothers and sisters.

But trying to be "good Christians" in our own strength doesn't get us anywhere. "We are all infected and impure with sin. When we put on our prized robes of righteousness we find they are but filthy rags" (Isaiah 64:6, LB). Trying to clean up our own lives only makes a bigger mess. Only by letting Jesus Christ have control of our lives can we be clean before God and have peace with ourselves.

The issue is one of *lordship. Lord* means master or boss. Who's your boss? Are you willing to let Jesus Christ control every area of your life?

The Apostle Paul expressed what it means to let Jesus have full control. Paul wrote: "I have been crucified with Christ and I no longer live, but Christ lives in me. The life I live in the body, I live by faith in the Son of God, who loved me and gave Himself for me" (Galatians 2:20).

Paul said that someone else—Jesus Christ—was now alive in his body. And about himself, Paul said, "I've been crucified. I'm dead."

Did that mean that Paul was physically dead? No. But the picture is clear. Paul meant that Jesus Christ was now controlling his life. Jesus was owner and master of the "house" that Paul used to control.

The Big I

It's interesting to notice how many times Paul uses the word "I" in that verse (Galatians 2:20): "*I* have been crucified"; "*I* no longer live"; "the life *I* now live, *I* live by faith." Paul recognized that the basic problem all people have is selfishness—the *Big I.* "*I* want what *I* want, when *I* want it!"

Have you ever noticed the first thing most people do when they get their school yearbooks? They start leafing through to find their favorite teacher's picture, right? Or their best friend's? No way! They whip through that yearbook looking for their own picture.

Some people even scrawl a big red circle around their picture every time they find it. They want to make sure their smile is right, their hair straight, that they look good.

People are basically selfish. They're concerned with the Big I. And that preoccupation with themselves causes lots of problems.

One problem is *rebellion*. Many people are like the guy who was always fighting with his parents. One day he and his father had been hassling back and forth for about an hour, and both were at the boiling point, about to explode. Finally, the son yelled, "I didn't ask to be born, you know!" The father snapped back, "If you had asked, the answer would have been *no!*"

Another Big I problem is that of *bad attitudes*. Bad attitudes usually result from pride. Take the guy who can't stand to be wrong. The teacher asks him, "What is two plus two?" The guy answers, "Five." When the teacher says he's wrong, the student tries to convince her that, "according to the *new* math," the answer really is five. The guy has a problem!

Another bad attitude expresses itself in conceit—the girl who thinks she's God's great gift to the male sex, for example. Still another person seems to have the opposite problem. She's got a poor self-image: "Nobody likes me. Nobody wants to be around me."

The interesting point is that both of these people have the same root problem. One expresses it in conceit, the other by being overly concerned about what others think about her. But both girls are totally into themselves. Both are captives of the Big I.

Self Spelled S-I-N

The Big I problem is really the age-old problem
that the Bible calls *sin*. What is sin? One way it
can be defined, according to the Bible, is "missing
the mark." The idea expressed in this definition
is of someone shooting an arrow that falls short of
its target. "For all have sinned and *fall short* of
the glory of God" (Romans 3:23, *italics mine*).

Sin can also be defined as "stepping across the
line between right and wrong." "We all, like sheep,
have gone astray, each of us has turned to his own
way" (Isaiah 53:6). That's sin too—going our own
way, the wrong way, instead of God's way.

The Bible also defines sin as "lawlessness."
"Everyone who sins breaks the law; in fact, sin is
lawlessness" (1 John 3:4). When a person does his
own thing, knowing it is contrary to God's way,
that is sin.

Taken together, these three definitions provide
a picture of what it means to sin. But the picture
is incomplete, because sin is more than something
you do; it's also what *causes* you to do wrong. It's
something *internal*.

The nature of sin is selfishness. It's an inside
condition that leads to outside actions. It is self—
the Big I—controlling one's life instead of God.

With the Big I in control, we're like a breed of
monkeys that lives in the South Sea Islands. Leave
a small cage with a banana inside it near one of
these monkeys. The monkey pokes its arm into
the cage and grabs the banana.

If the bars of the cage are far enough apart to
allow the monkey to bring the banana back
through, there's no problem. But if the bars are so

close together that the monkey can't bring its fistful of fruit back out, the animal is trapped. It wants the banana so badly that it won't drop the banana and bring its arm out empty-handed. Monkeys have been known to die with their greedy fists stuck in the cage.

For the greedy-fisted monkeys, the solution to their problem is simple. Drop the banana. God has a solution for our sin problem too. It's a solution that deals with the Big I.

The Dead I

"I have been crucified with Christ . . ."

Jesus used a simple illustration to explain what happens when we die to the Big I. He said, "Unless a kernel of wheat falls to the ground and dies, it remains only a single seed. But if it dies, it produces many seeds. The man who loves his life will lose it, while the man who hates his life in this world will keep it for eternal life" (John 12:24-25).

Most people in Jesus' day lived on or near farms. They understood exactly what Jesus was talking about when He referred to the process of growing wheat. The farmer had to plant the kernel in the ground and leave it. In the damp soil, the seed began to decompose. The entire kernel "died"—except for one tiny part called the *germ*.

While the rest of the seed was decomposing, the germ began to grow. It actually nourished itself from the decomposed seed. Eventually the germ grew strong enough to send out shoots into the ground and get its nourishment from the earth.

Unseen by human eyes, the process of germination continued in the silent earth. Then one day a green shoot burst out of the ground. Day by day it grew till it was a mature, healthy wheat plant. The mature plant contained hundreds of new kernels of its own, each full of tremendous potential for growth.

This whole growth process began with a decision on the part of the farmer. He had to decide whether to hold on to the single wheat kernel, and get nothing out of it, or bury the kernel in the earth and let it die, eventually to get a new crop.

In the same way, the person who lives for himself loses in the end. But the person who gives up his own desires and lets Jesus take control really starts to live.

The world says, "Get all you can for the Big I." "Go for the gusto!" Jesus says, "If you cling to your life, you will lose it; but if you give it up for Me, you will save it" (Matthew 10:39, LB).

Jesus wants our lives to be fulfilling. He said, "My purpose is to give life in all its fullness" (John 10:10, LB). If we are willing to give our lives up to Him, then He can help us reach our full potential. But we must die to the Big I—surrender control of our lives to Him.

The Christ-controlled I

"I no longer live, but Christ lives in me."

During my senior year in college, one of the guys who lived on my dorm floor got drunk. Normally, he was one of the nicest people I knew. But this weekend was different. He'd had an ar-

gument with his girlfriend, so he got blasted, stag-
gered into his room, and started smashing things.

Finally it became necessary to restrain him. The
guy was a football player who weighed 230 pounds
and stood 6'5". It took 10 men to hold him
down.

Sober, the guy was mild-mannered and polite.
Drunk, he was an animal. Under the control of
alcohol, his personality completely changed.

Just as alcohol can control people in a negative
way, so Jesus Christ can control us in a positive
way. That is probably why the Apostle Paul used
drinking wine as an illustration of how Christ's
control of our lives works. "And be not drunk with
wine, wherein is excess; but be filled with the
Spirit" (Ephesians 5:18, KJV). The Greek word
translated "filled" means "to control." When Jesus
takes control of our lives, He smashes old habits.
He fills us with joy, peace, and power.

But sometimes we ask Christ to take control of
our lives, and He does, then later we realize that
we are back in control again. We have resisted the
Lord's direction and started to run our own lives
once more.

The good news is that God provides a way for
us to let the Spirit control us again. That way is
expressed in a little formula: *confession + control
= victory*.

Confession. We confess to the Lord that we have
sinned. "If we confess our sins, He is faithful and
just and will forgive us our sins and purify us from
all unrighteousness" (1 John 1:9).

Control. Forgiveness is wonderful. But that is
only one part of the formula. The other part is
claiming by faith the control of the Holy Spirit.

Once sin is confessed God is anxious to fill us with His Spirit.

The following illustration has helped me a lot. Several times every minute, we exhale air that's full of carbon dioxide. Then we inhale air containing a high oxygen content. The used-up air, the carbon dioxide, goes out; the new breath of oxygen comes in. The bad goes out; the good comes in.

That is the way to experience the lordship of Jesus. Moment by moment, we "breathe" out any sin and selfishness. Then we "breathe" in the life of Jesus, His Holy Spirit.

It's a matter of believing what the Bible says—that the Big I has been crucified—then trusting Jesus, moment by moment, to live His life through us by the Holy Spirit.

Living under His lordship involves a positive as well as a negative aspect. We *die* to the Big I, but we *come alive* to God through Jesus Christ. We turn our backs on sin, but we receive—through simple faith—all the joy, power, and abundant life that only Jesus Christ can give.

A lot of people get caught up in the negative aspect—no to this, no to that. What a down way to live. While we should say *no* to sin and selfishness, we can say *yes* to all that Jesus Christ is. A death is involved, but there's life—abundant, resurrection life—on the other side!

Getting to know Jesus—it requires an understanding of who He is and why He came and died and rose again. Then a relationship with Him can begin to develop when we receive Him into our lives. But it doesn't stop there. Knowing Jesus is a lifetime process. It involves a relationship that grows as we let Him be Lord of our lives, and as we experience His lordship in every area of our lives.

7

Lord of Priorities

The tiny aircraft, tied down with ropes, swayed back and forth in the wind. My first sight of the little private plane did nothing to ease my fears.

A man I knew who owned the plane, had offered to fly my friend Rod and me from Oklahoma City to Albuquerque. Neither of us had ever flown on anything smaller than a DC-10, so we were nervous about traveling in a small plane. But we accepted the invitation.

I watched the plane being loaded and it seemed to sink a little closer to the ground each time another piece of luggage went on board. Rod climbed into the back seat and I sat up front. As the plane *put-putted* down the runway, the thought occurred to me: *This is nothing but a Volkswagen with wings!* But it was too late to back out.

In spite of my worries, once we got into the air I began to enjoy myself. The Oklahoma country-side stretched out below us, and the view was fantastic. I passed the time by asking the pilot about the instruments in the plane.

We had been in the air for about an hour when my pilot friend asked me, "Hey, Barry, how would you like to fly this thing?"

"You mean the plane? Me?"

"Yeah." He shoved the movable steering wheel over to me. The plane began to wobble back and forth, and it suddenly got super quiet in the backseat where Rod was sitting. As the pilot gave me instructions, I steered the plane to the left, then to the right. Finally, I got it back under control.

Suddenly, a huge cloud bank loomed ahead. I tried to sound casual as I asked, "Should we go over, under, or around it?"

"Right on through," the pilot answered.

I had learned in grade school what a cloud is— "an airborne mass of water particles." But at that moment all I could think of was, *WALL! We're going to hit it!* Instead, we eased into the cloud bank and lost all visibility. We couldn't even see the wings on either side of the plane.

The plane began to pitch around, and I suddenly had no sense of where we were—up, down, or sideways. I looked back at my friend Rod just in time to see him groping for the little brown sick bag.

At that point, my pilot friend grabbed the controls. "St. Clair," he said matter-of-factly, "you don't know which end is up."

Living Right-side-up

For many people, their lives are like that plane ride—they don't know which end is up. The reason is they have never determined what is really important in life. They live life with no clear-cut priorities to provide meaning and direction.

Other people have some priorities, but their priorities are wrong. What's most important to them is a girlfriend or a boyfriend, getting their own car, or being popular. That's not to say that it's wrong to want these things. But when people make them the most important things in their lives, it indicates that their priorities are off. They will wind up lost in the clouds.

Christians as well as non-Christians have problems with priorities. We Christians often come up with nice, spiritual-sounding phrases like "doing God's will" or "putting God first." But our lives show that our top priorities are making first team, or making all As, or being accepted by a certain group.

Our real priorities are the ones which hold our affections and to which we give our energies. These priorities, not the ones we mouth with our lips, determine the direction of our lives.

Jesus Christ has told us what things are really important. The question is, are we willing to find out how His priorities compare with ours? Are we willing to let Him be Lord of our priorities?

"One of the teachers of the Law came and heard them debating. Noticing that Jesus had given them a good answer, he asked Him, 'Of all the commandments, which is the most important?'

"'The most important one,' answered Jesus, 'is this: "Hear, O Israel, The Lord our God, is one. Love the Lord your God with all your heart and with all your soul and with all your mind and with all your strength." The second is this: "Love your neighbor as yourself." There is no commandment greater than these' " (Mark 12:28-31).

In this Scripture, Jesus gives three top priorities for our lives. What's most important, He says, is to *(1) love God, (2) love your neighbor, and (3) love yourself*. Let's consider these three priorities in reverse order.

Love Yourself

I have known some young people who can hardly wait to wake up every morning and look at themselves in the mirror. They think they are the most adorable creatures to come along since "Miss Piggy" joined the Muppets. That kind of love does not represent what Jesus meant by loving yourself.

But the fact is, I don't know many teenagers who love themselves too much. Most of the teens who I know really don't like themselves very much. In fact, a survey published a few years ago by the Institute on Basic Youth Conflicts indicated that 95 percent of American high school students don't like themselves.

You can probably identify in some way with the feelings of that 95 percent. Maybe it's your looks you don't like. You think your nose is too big. You feel your legs are too skinny. You walk into the bathroom, squeeze a few zits and say, "What a creep! What a creep!"

Maybe you don't like yourself because you feel you don't have any ability. You think that when God passed out talent, you got shafted. Or you don't like your family background. Your house is too small compared with your friends'. Your parents don't dress right.

We need to understand what Jesus meant by "loving yourself." The last chapter talked about "dying to self." Now we are talking about "loving yourself." Sound contradictory? Obviously, Jesus doesn't mean that we are supposed to be conceited or hung up on ourselves. He means that we are to *accept ourselves*. Jesus wants us to accept the way He made us, and to realize that we are important to Him.

Many of us, if we're honest, feel that God blew it when He made us. But the truth, as hard as it may be to believe, is that Jesus thinks you and I are important. And He loves us—just the way we are—crooked teeth, pimples, skinny legs, and all! We were made for a specific purpose. God has a plan for our lives.

But what happens when we don't accept ourselves? First, we start accepting the moral values of people around us. Subconsciously we think, "He is sharper, smarter, and better than me, so what He does must be OK." As a result, if that person goes out to get drunk, we go too.

A second result of not accepting ourselves is that we get mad at God. "God made a mess out of me," we reason. "Why should I mess with Him?"

If Jesus is your Lord, you are committed to following His priorities. Those priorities include "loving yourself." How can you overcome negative feelings about yourself and experience self-acceptance?

● *Realize that God made you according to His plan. He didn't make a mistake!* "You saw me before I was born and scheduled each day of my life before I began to breathe. Every day was recorded in Your Book!" (Psalm 139:16, LB)

• *Don't compare yourself with others.* "We do not dare to classify or compare ourselves with some who commend themselves. When they measure themselves by themselves and compare themselves with themselves, they are not wise" (2 Corinthians 10:12).

• *Realize that God is more concerned with inner qualities than with your outward appearance.* "The Lord does not look at the things man looks at. Man looks at the outward appearance, but the Lord looks at the heart" (1 Samuel 16:7).

• *Cooperate with God as He continues your development.* "For we are God's workmanship, created in Christ Jesus to do good works, which God prepared in advance for us to do" (Ephesians 2:10).

• *Begin to develop a "healthy countenance."* Your countenance is the expression on your face that reveals the inner condition of your heart. "O my soul, why be so gloomy and discouraged? Trust in God! I shall again praise Him for His wondrous help, He will make me smile again, *for He is my God!*" (Psalm 43:5, LB)

• *Recognize your weaknesses and let God use them as strengths.* "But He said to me, 'My grace is sufficient for you, for My power is made perfect in weakness.' Therefore I will boast all the more gladly about my weaknesses, so that Christ's power may rest on me" (2 Corinthians 12:9).

• *Let God make you into the best person you can be.* "And so, dear brothers, I plead with you to give your bodies to God. Let them be a living sacrifice, holy—the kind He can accept. When you think of what He has done for you, is this too much to ask? Don't copy the behavior and customs of this world, but be a new and different person, with a fresh newness in all you do and think. Then you will learn from your own experience how His way will really satisfy you" (Romans 12:1-2, LB).

Remember the sign outside the old store: "God don't make no junk!" God made you to be a person of tremendous value. Accept yourself!

Love Your Neighbor

Jesus gave a second priority: "Love your neighbor. . . ." This command has become a familiar cliché. It's so familiar that often we don't even think about what it means.

In his book, *Born Again*, Charles Colson tells a true story that dramatically demonstrates what it means to love your neighbor. Colson, part of the White House inner circle with Richard Nixon, was convicted for his part in the Watergate scandal, and was eventually sent to prison.

But just before Watergate broke, Colson received a "proper introduction" to Jesus Christ, and accepted Him as Lord. During the scandal, a group of Christians befriended Colson. Their names were Fred Rhodes, Albert Quie, and Harold Hughes.

These were politicians, Democrats and Republicans. All of them had a lot to lose by remaining Colson's friends. But they stood by him through the trial with all its negative press coverage. They visited him in prison, and tried to encourage him in every way they could.

One day Colson received word that his son had been picked up on a drug charge. He wanted desperately to get out of prison and return to his troubled family. But it didn't seem possible.

Then his friend Al Quie, a Christian congress-
man, called Colson and said, "Chuck, we've been
praying and thinking about what else we can do
to help you. There's an old statute that allows one
person or a group of people to take another man's
place in prison. The three of us are going to pe-
tition the judge to let us take your place."

As it turned out, the situation improved without
Quie, Rhodes, or Hughes being jailed. But the fact
remains: These three men, who had every reason
to reject Colson, were willing to go to prison so
that he could be with his family. That's loving
your neighbor!

Most of us would admit that we are not quite
that unselfish. Sometimes we say we love people
when we are really just looking for what we can
get from them. Selfishness prevents us from really
loving our neighbor.

Fear of rejection is another obstacle which keeps
us from loving people. We are constantly wondering, "What does he really think of me? I hope she
will like me, but she probably won't." Our fear of
being rejected causes us to be defensive. It causes
us to protect ourselves rather than *give* of
ourselves.

There is a way of viewing people that can help
overcome selfishness, fear of rejection, and the
other obstacles that keep us from loving. It involves seeing every contact with another person
as a *divine encounter*. That means realizing that
God brings people into contact with us for specific
reasons. Because of that realization we can ask,
"Lord, what are You doing in this person's life?
How do You want to use me in his life?"

Seeing our day-to-day contacts as divine encounters motivates us to take an interest in people. It challenges us to accept people and to respect their self-worth.

This is not something that we learn overnight. But with the Lord's help, we can learn to view every contact with people as a divine encounter. We can learn to love our neighbor—whether it's someone we love being with, or the classmate with bad breath and B.O. And the best place to begin is with those closest to us—our parents, brothers, and sisters.

Here's what the Apostle Paul had to say about having the right attitude toward others: "Don't be selfish; don't live to make a good impression on others. Be humble, thinking of others as better than yourself. Don't just think about your own affairs, but be interested in others, too, and in what they are doing" (Philippians 2:3-4, LB).

Love God

A third top priority for our lives concerns our love for God. It is the most significant priority of all. Jesus said, "Love the Lord your God with all your heart and with all your soul and with all your mind and with all your strength" (Mark 12:30).

A love relationship is a two-way street. Imagine that you are dating someone whom you care for a lot. For a long time, you've been afraid to say how you really feel. But one night you muster all the courage you can find and blurt out, "I love you!" Then your date turns to you and calmly replies, "Stick it in your ear." Obviously, you don't have much of a relationship with that person.

God has taken the initiative in developing a relationship with us. The Cross proves just how much He loves us: "But God demonstrates His own love for us in this: While we were still sinners, Christ died for us" (Romans 5:8). The next step is ours.

How, then, can we return God's love? According to Mark 12:30, we are to love Him with all our heart, with all our soul, with all our mind, and with all our strength.

Loving God "with all your heart" means that you turn your emotions over to Jesus Christ. It means that you commit your affections to Him in such a way that nothing or no one means more to you than the Lord.

Loving God "with all your soul" means loving Him with your total personality—your actions, your attitudes, your habits.

Loving God "with all your mind" involves a commitment of your intellect. It means focusing your thoughts on the Lord and on His Word. It means allowing the Lord to change your thought patterns so that your thought life can please Him.

Loving God "with all your strength" means that you love Him with your "will." It means choosing to follow the Lord's way in every situation, even when you face resistance.

It's like a weight lifter. He yanks the barbell from the floor to his chest. Then, trembling under the weight, he gives one gut-wrenching push and lifts the barbell over his head. Every ounce of effort goes into moving that barbell from the floor to the top of the weight lifter's reach. That's a picture of what it means to love God with all your strength.

Loving God often involves cold-blooded obedience, doing what we know is right even though we don't feel like doing it. Jesus said, "Whoever has My commandments and obeys them, he is the one who loves Me. He who loves Me will be loved by My Father, and I too will love him and show Myself to him" (John 14:21).

Loving God costs something. For example, it may mean getting out of bed 20 minutes earlier to spend time with the Lord. Maybe you have decided that you want to have morning devotions, but somehow at 6:30 A.M., getting up doesn't make any sense. I'd like to believe that, right then, God is saying to some of His angels, "Hey, get busy! There's one of My children. He's really trying to please Me."

One thing for sure, God knows when we're trying to grow in our love for Him. And He even gives us the strength we need to really love Him!

What's Important?

This chapter began by asking, "What is really important in life?" How we answer that question will determine the direction of our lives here on earth, and in eternity.

Years ago two young men, Adoniram Judson and Jacob Eames, were students at Providence College, now called Brown University. Judson had come from a Christian home, but rejected the Christian faith. Through the influence of his friend Eames, Judson became a deist.

Deism is the belief that God, or some supreme being, created the world, then wound it up like a clock and left it to run by itself. In other words, though God may exist, He has little to do with people's lives. Deism denies man's need for a personal relationship with God through Jesus Christ.

During their college years, Eames and Judson preached their philosophy of do-it-yourself living. They encouraged people to give up the idea of a personal God who answered prayer.

After college the two young men went their separate ways. Judson was unusually brilliant, and obtained a position as a college professor.

One time, while traveling, Judson stayed in the home of a preacher who spoke to him about the Gospel of Jesus Christ. The following evening, Judson stopped at a roadside inn to spend the night.

"You probably won't want to stay," he was told. Only one room was vacant and it was located next to a room where a man was dying. The man was disturbing hotel guests with his agonizing screams.

Nevertheless, Judson decided to stay at the inn. During the night he was awakened by the dying man's screams. As Judson lay awake listening, he became troubled by the thought of facing his own death—and eternity.

He tried to sluff off the worrisome thoughts. *What if Jacob Eames could see me now?* Judson asked himself. *What would he think? He would probably have a good laugh, at my expense.* Judson pulled the covers up around him and went back to sleep.

When he payed his bill the next morning, he asked the innkeeper about the man in the next room. The innkeeper told Judson that the man had died during the night. Almost without thinking, Judson asked, "Who was he?"

"Eames . . . Jacob Eames," the innkeeper replied.

In shock, Judson walked outside and rode off on his horse. Deism, Judson realized, didn't have the answers about life and death after all. He began trying to discover what was really important in life. A short time later, Adoniram Judson received Jesus Christ and committed his life to Him. He began learning to love God, to love his neighbor, and to love himself.

As a result, God used Judson in tremendous ways. He became the father of modern missions, and God used him to challenge thousands of Americans to become missionaries. Judson himself became a missionary to Burma where he served for over 30 years. Adoniram Judson discovered what's really important in life.

8

Lord of Attitudes

Start-of-the-season football practice. . . . Swelter-
ing August heat. Aching bodies. Sweat-soaked jer-
seys. Blocks. Tackles. Groans. And lots of *bad*
attitudes.

As chaplain of the Avondale High football team,
I attended those grueling, two-a-day drills nearly
every day. Sometimes when the players came near
the edge of the field, I could hear them muttering
and complaining. Near the end of practice, when
the coach lined them up for wind sprints, I could
hear what those guys were saying about him.

He would blow his whistle, and a line of grass-
stained bodies would jerk into gear. No sooner
had they hit full-stride, than the coach would *tweet*
his whistle again. And the players would turn
around and run back. Back and forth, up and down
the field they would run—till they nearly dropped.

Judging by the comments I overheard, most of
those players wished they could have a turn with
that little whistle. What they wanted to do was
blow it in the coach's ear till his eardrum burst,

and run him up and down the field till his tongue dragged the ground! I mean there were some *bad* attitudes on that field.

But 14 weeks later I watched those guys lift the coach up on their shoulders and carry him across that same field. The team had just ended the season with a perfect, 14-0 record. They were the new state champions. And there had been some dramatic changes in those players' attitudes.

There is a spiritual lesson here for those who want to see it. God wants to change our attitudes— toward parents, toward circumstances, toward God—so we can be winners. Those changes are sometimes humbling, and often painful. But they are a necessary part of our spiritual growth. We can't become winners in God's kingdom unless we let Jesus be Lord of our attitudes.

Knowing what kinds of attitudes the Lord wants us to have is simple. He has told us very plainly:

"Have this attitude in yourselves which was also in Christ Jesus, who, although He existed in the form of God, did not regard equality with God a thing to be grasped, but emptied Himself, taking the form of a bond-servant, and being made in the likeness of men. And being found in appearance as a man, He humbled Himself by becoming obedient to the point of death, even death on a cross.

Therefore also God highly exalted Him, and bestowed on Him the name which is above every name, that at the name of Jesus every knee should bow, of those who are in heaven, and on earth, and under the earth, and that every tongue should confess that Jesus Christ is Lord, to the glory of God the Father" (Philippians 2:5-11, NASB).

This passage reveals three basic attitudes that

characterized Jesus' life: *(1) He refused to hold onto selfish ambition. (2) He gave up His rights in order to serve others. (3) He humbled Himself in order to become obedient.* As a result of Jesus' attitudes (and actions), God the Father "exalted Him." God made Him a winner. And He wants to do the same with you.

Success—Yours or His?

Jesus refused to hold on to selfish ambition. He was equal to God. He had the same nature as God. But He didn't hold on to that power and prestige. Instead, He "emptied Himself" (Philippians 2:7).

What did it mean for Jesus to empty Himself? Imagine a full glass of water, then think of it being turned over and poured out. In a similar way, Jesus poured out any personal ambitions He might have had. He poured out all of the glory that was His as a result of being equal with God the Father. Jesus emptied Himself so that He could be completely filled with what His Father wanted.

Jesus' life is a model for our lives. God wants us to pour out those things that we hold onto in order to "be somebody." He wants us to be emptied of our own selfish goals and ambitions. Then He can pour into us His goals for our lives.

One of the biggest struggles I've had in my own life has been with my desire for success and recognition. I have always wanted people to approve of me, to accept me, and like me.

Time after time, God has had to deal with my attitudes in this area. In one period of my life, I came to a point where I had to face up to some areas of personal failure and defeat. Nobody likes to fail. But I realized that the reason these failures were troubling me so much was because my attitude was wrong. I was disobeying the Bible's command to "do nothing out of selfish ambition or vain conceit" (Philippians 2:3).

As I thought and prayed about this problem, I realized that I needed to turn some things over to God. I wrote in my diary:

> I give in. I give up. I lay down my hopes, my dreams, my ambitions for success. I lay down my reputation, my respectability among my peers, my approval among those from whom I want approval. I give them all up to You, Lord.
>
> Amen.

That prayer described the way I felt at the moment about my selfish ambitions. I began to realize that God is much more interested in whether we obey and follow Him than whether we succeed.

Most people have problems with "selfish ambition and vain conceit." We strive, out of selfishness, for grades, for popularity, for the approval of friends. It's all too easy to make success a goal that we place ahead of God and His plan for us.

Jesus did not base His life on selfish ambitions. His one ambition was to please His Father.

When Rights Are Wrong

Jesus gave up His rights in order to serve others. He took on Himself "the very nature of a servant"

(Philippians 2:7). If anyone had "rights," it was the Lord of the universe. But Jesus gave up His rights in order to become a servant.

"Whoever wants to be great among you must be your servant, and whoever wants to be first must be slave of all. For even the Son of Man did not come to be served, but to serve, and to give His life as a ransom for many" (Mark 10:43-45).

"Hey! This soup is cold!"

"Get out of here and don't come back. This is *my* room!"

"That stupid teacher! She doesn't have any right to tell me that!"

"That's my new flannel shirt! Just because Brian is my brother doesn't give him the right to wear it!"

Sound familiar?

The world tells us to fight for what we can get for ourselves. But God has a better way. He tells us to give up our rights and learn to serve, instead of worrying about getting "what's rightfully mine."

To learn how to be a servant, the best place to start is with your parents. That may be the one area where you would like most to hold on to your rights. In many ways, it is harder to develop a servant's attitude with your parents than in any other relationship. But if you learn servanthood there, you really learn it.

Jesus was the greatest example of servanthood that ever lived. He served us *all* by the way He gave up His life. But His first priority was to serve His Father.

God has given your parents to you. You can respond to them in one of two ways. You can rebel against them and demand your "rights," which is contrary to the attitude of Jesus Christ. Or you can submit to them and let Jesus make something beautiful out of your relationship. This second response is contrary to the world's way. It's not popular or easy. But it is Jesus' way.

Here's an example.

Don has just gotten his driver's license, and he asks his dad if he can use the family car. His dad says, "Yes, Son, you can use it. But I would like for you to wash it first."

"Oh, man," Don responds, "I can't believe you would ask me to do that. I've got to go to the church and be spiritual. And I've got all these other things I want to do. Why can't you just take it to the car wash? I mean . . . never mind! I'll get a ride with somebody!"

Then while Don is in his room hyperventilating, his dad is thinking, *I guess he's still pretty immature. I'd like to let him use the car, but maybe it's not a good idea—at least till he grows up some more.*

Now let's turn the situation around. Don asks for the car, and his dad says, "OK, but wash it first."

Don says, "Sure, I'll wash it." He washes the car, waxes it, and puts gas in it—with his own money no less!

Guess how Don's dad responds: *Ah, yes, the kid's growing up. He's starting to be responsible. I think I'll tell him he can have the car next weekend too.* It was Don's attitude that made all the difference.

If you want Jesus to be Lord of your attitudes, start putting the following steps into practice as you relate to your parents:

(1) Try to see life from your parents' perspective. Did you ever consider the fact that your dad (and perhaps your mother too) is committed to a job that he goes to day after day, and that sometimes it's not very fulfilling? Do you realize that your parents may be trying to sort through a conflict between themselves, and may be having a tough time getting things worked out?

Have you ever thought that your dad may be going through a "mid-life crisis"? (That means he's reached a stage in life where he knows he won't live forever and he's wondering if his life is really worth much.) Do you know that sometimes your mother feels lonely and unappreciated?

If you want Jesus to be Lord of your attitudes, start trying to see life from your parents' perspective. Then learn to meet some of their needs—for understanding, appreciation, love—instead of demanding that they always serve you.

(2) Ask your parents for advice. "Wait a minute!" someone objects. "I'm just starting to make my own decisions. If I ask my parents for advice, I'll just be back under their thumbs."

Not necessarily. It takes maturity to *voluntarily* ask people for advice (and even greater maturity to accept advice). Your parents know that. They will respect you for asking, and will probably give you more freedom because of the maturity you've demonstrated.

Maybe your parents don't want to pry into your affairs, so they don't ask many questions. But you can be sure they would like to be a greater part of your life. You can open up communication by asking their opinions about your future, your friends, decisions you have to make. Again, it's a matter of attitude. The prideful person runs from advice. The humble person asks for it.

(3) *Show your appreciation.* Sometime, take your parents out for a nice dinner and pay for it. That's one way to show you appreciate them. A more practical way is to help around the house—clean your room, pick up your clothes. That may sound corny, but it takes a real servant's heart to show appreciation in such practical, nitty-gritty acts of service.

(4) *Pray for your parents.* It would probably be a shock for many to know how few Christian young people pray regularly for their parents. Your parents need your prayers. Praying for them is an important way you can serve them.

(5) *Ask for forgiveness.* Maybe relating to your parents with the attitude of a servant seems totally unrealistic. There are just too many hurts, too many bad feelings between you. In that case, the first step you may need to take is to ask forgiveness— first God's, then your parents'.

Don't let the fact that they also have been wrong stand in your way. Confess to them your own wrong attitudes and actions. Be specific. Then ask, "Will you forgive me?"

Asking forgiveness will be hard. But it could be one of the greatest steps you have ever taken. Forgiveness is God's way of healing relationships.

(6) *Tell your parents you love them.* How long has it been?

Maybe you are thinking, "I want to have the attitude of a servant, like Jesus. In fact, I've tried to have it. But I don't know whether or not I've learned to be a servant." You can know whether you have the attitude of a servant by the way you respond when people treat you like a servant. How do you respond when your parents ask you to do "dumb" things that maybe you don't think even need to be done? Do you demand your rights? Or do you give them up to God?

Having the attitude of a servant is something that has to be learned. Don't be discouraged if you struggle with wrong attitudes in this area. Everyone does. But do give serious consideration to the question, "Am I willing to give up my rights in order to serve others?"

Willing to Obey

"Then Jesus brought them to a garden grove, Gethsemane, and told them to sit down and wait while He went ahead to pray. He took Peter with Him and Zebedee's two sons, James and John, and began to be filled with anguish and despair.

"Then He told them, 'My soul is crushed with horror and sadness to the point of death . . . stay here . . . stay awake with Me.'

"He went forward a little, and fell face downward on the ground, and prayed, 'My Father! If it is possible, let this cup be taken away from Me. But I want Your will, not Mine' " (Matthew 26:36-39, LB).

That night in the garden, Jesus knew what lay ahead for Him. He knew what it would mean to be nailed to a cross and to take on Himself all the sins of mankind.

Emotionally He was torn up inside. He moved from rock to rock saying, "Father, if there is any way out of this, I want out." But then He told His Father, "It's not what I want but what You want that is really important."

The Apostle Paul put it this way: "He humbled Himself and became obedient to death—even death on a cross!" (Philippians 2:8) *Jesus' attitude was one of humility which produced obedience to the Father's will.*

How's your attitude in this area? Are you willing to obey the Lord no matter what the cost? It cost Jesus His life. It may cost you friends, time, hopes, dreams. . . . It may even cost you your life to have the kind of attitude that produces obedience to Jesus Christ.

Is it worth the cost?

The Price and the Prize

Remember the Avondale football team? Was the price those players payed—the sweat, the pain, the hard work—worth it? After the 14-0 season, I attended a banquet for the team. I don't know whether the players even thought about those two-a-day August practices as they celebrated together. But if they did, I think they would have said, "It was worth it!"

Was it worth it for Jesus? Paul wrote:
"Therefore God exalted Him to the highest place and gave Him the name that is above every name, that at the name of Jesus every knee should bow, in heaven and on earth, and every tongue confess that Jesus Christ is Lord, to the glory of God the Father" (Philippians 2:9-11).

Is it worth it for the Christian who lays his life

down to follow Jesus? Peter wrote, "If you will humble yourselves under the mighty hand of God, in His good time He will lift you up" (1 Peter 5:6, LB).

God takes us through some hard times in order to make us winners. Before the Resurrection there had to be a Cross. Anyone who seriously considers allowing Jesus to be Lord of his life should be prepared to learn humility. But God promises that if we humble ourselves, He will lift us up.

At that football banquet, the whole team as well as individual players were presented with trophies. A trophy is a reflection of someone's accomplishments. When we allow Jesus to put His attitudes in us, we become His trophies. Jesus Himself is reflected in our lives so that He can say of us, "He's one of My trophies. He's a reflection of Me."

Jesus' attitudes in us reflect out to others: "But we Christians have no veil over our faces; we can be mirrors that brightly reflect the glory of the Lord. And as the Spirit of the Lord works within us, we become more and more like Him" (2 Corinthians 3:18, LB).

When we have His attitudes—refusing to hold onto selfish ambitions, giving up our rights in order to serve others, and humbling ourselves in order to become obedient—He can lift us up, and place us in His trophy case for the world to see.

9

Lord Over Temptation

The final soccer game of the season is over and Brian is driving around with some of his teammates. Somebody says, "Let's celebrate!" And the van stops at a liquor store. Brian is trying to think of a cool way to refuse, when someone tosses a cool one into his lap. *TEMPTATION!*

It's the first chance John has had to drive his father's car. He's been itching to try it out. It is late and there is no traffic. And after all, John reasons, the speedometer does go to 160 mph. *TEMPTATION!*

The kids are asleep. It's a bad night for TV and Karen doesn't feel like studying. Baby-sitting never seemed more boring. Then the phone rings. It's Karen's boyfriend and he wants to come over. But she knows that the people she's sitting for have a rule: "no boys in the house." The voice at the other end of the phone asks hopefully, "Well, can I come?"

TEMPTATION! How does it begin? Does God cause it? How do you handle it?

"The Devil Made Me Do It"

One of the key Scriptures concerning temptation is found in the Book of James: "When tempted, no one should say 'God is tempting me.' For God cannot be tempted by evil, nor does He tempt anyone; but each one is tempted when, by his own evil desire, he is dragged away and enticed. Then, after desire has conceived, it gives birth to sin; and sin, when it is full-grown, gives birth to death" (James 1:13-15).

God doesn't tempt anyone. So who does? The Apostle Peter wrote, "Be self-controlled and alert. Your enemy the devil prowls around like a roaring lion looking for someone to devour" (1 Peter 5:8).

Satan is the source of temptation. His goal has always been to keep people separated from God. First he tries to keep us from receiving Christ. When that fails, he tries to prevent us from letting Jesus control our lives.

Since Satan is the source of temptation, we can't blame God. But we can't lay all the blame on Satan either. "The devil made me do it" is a half-truth at best. "Each one is tempted when, *by his own evil desire*, he is dragged away and enticed" (James 1:14, *italics mine*). Satan is able to tempt us only because he is able to appeal to some desire within us.

If I am trying to lose weight and someone offers me some food that I really don't like, I'm not tempted at all. But if someone offers me a big, luscious piece of chocolate cake—that's a temptation!

Sometimes, temptation appeals to good, God-given desires that become misdirected. Satan tempts us to fulfill them in ways contrary to God's way. For example, the desire for sex is a God-given desire—perfectly normal and healthy. But Satan tempts us with sex when he tries to get us to have sex with someone we're not married to.

So, the first element in the temptation process is *Satan*, the source of temptation. The second element is a *desire* of some kind. The third element is an *enticement*, some attraction outside of ourselves. "Each one is tempted when, by his own evil desire, he is dragged away and *enticed* (James 1:14, *italics mine*).

Consider the following "fishy" illustration: A young fish is swimming in a pond. Father fish has warned him to stay away from any worms that might be hanging around on strings.

One day the young fish swims past a worm and notices how luscious it looks dangling there in the water. The fish swims on, remembering Father fish's warning. But the memory of that juicy worm lingers, and the young fish swims back for another look. Again, he manages to tear himself away without taking a bite. But he can't get the picture of that worm out of his mind.

He keeps hanging around, looking at the worm. Finally, the fish can't take it any longer. He chomps down on the bait and, sure enough, a hook rips through his mouth and he's pulled away.

The fisherman uses worms for a reason. He knows that inside every fish is a desire for worms. So the fisherman uses the appropriate bait as an enticement.

The same thing happens to people. We start hanging around whatever it is that tempts us. Then we begin to actively pursue it, because we have become convinced that having it will mean "satisfaction guaranteed."

For example, a guy and girl have promised each other that they are not going to get physically involved. But they check in at their school's favorite parking place "just to see who's there." Being close feels so good. And one thing leads to another. . . . They've been *enticed*.

Birth, Growth, Death

The *birth of sin* is the fourth element in the temptation process (unless, of course, the sin is resisted). Satan, the source of temptation, arranges for an enticement to appeal to some desire within us. Then, if we take the bait, the hook sinks in.

It is important to understand that sin does not take place till "the bait is swallowed." *It's not a sin to be tempted.* Even Jesus was tempted. In fact, He was tempted in many of the same ways we are. But He never sinned (Hebrews 4:15).

James wrote: "Then, after desire has conceived, it *gives birth* to sin" (James 1:15, *italics mine*). Why does James use the figure of "birth"? When a woman gives birth to a child and the child is nourished, growth begins to take place. In the same way, when sin is born it begins to grow.

That leads us to the fifth element in the temptation process which is the *growth* of sin. A "newborn sin" grows into a "full-grown" sinful habit. For example: a few drinks turn into an alcohol problem. Going too far on a date turns into an uncontrollable pattern of sex sins. An experiment with drugs leads to addiction.

Temptation is not always one of the "biggies": alcohol, sex, or drugs. Sometimes it's the temptation to talk about someone behind his back or cheat on a test. Sometimes it's giving in to laziness or a bad temper.

There are all kinds of temptations. But once a person takes the bait, sin begins to grow. And if a person continues to give in to a particular sin, he becomes its slave.

The final element in the temptation process is *death*. "Then, after desire has conceived, it gives birth to sin, and sin, when it is full-grown, gives birth to *death*" (James 1:15, *italics mine*). Here, "death" refers to *spiritual* death.

What does it mean to be spiritually dead? When a person repeatedly gives in to temptation, he becomes hardened and insensitive to God. The Apostle Paul described a group of people who became so insensitive to God that He "gave them up" to sin (Romans 1:24, KJV).

It wasn't so much that God gave up on them as that they lost all sensitivity to Him. Their hearts were hard. Though alive physically, they were dead spiritually.

(Check out the temptation cycle diagram on page 105.)

Getting stuck on this merry-go-round brings disastrous results. It brings *defeat*, because of the inability to overcome temptation. It brings *spiritual immaturity*, because self is in control instead of Jesus. It brings *hypocrisy*, because Christianity is being faked instead of lived. And, ultimately, spiritual *death* is the result.

The good news is that God offers a way off the merry-go-round!

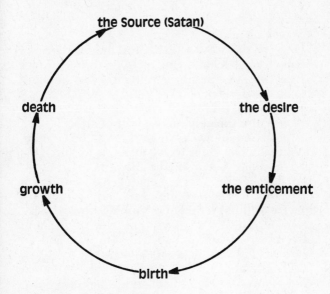

Count It Pure Joy

The Book of James, which tells so much about the process of temptation—how it works—also tells how to overcome it.

James wrote, "Consider it pure joy, my brothers, whenever you face trials of many kinds, because you know that the testing of your faith develops perseverance" (James 1:2).

Consider it joy? Why should we be joyful at a time when sin may be about to wipe us out? The answer is found in the verses that follow: "Because you know that the testing of your faith de-

velops perseverance. Perseverance must finish
its work so that you may be mature and complete,
not lacking anything" (James 1:3-4).

One of the ways God builds the character of
Jesus in us is by allowing us to go through times
of testing. As Satan tempts us, we become
stronger—*if* we don't give into temptation. So we
can "count it pure joy," knowing that the temptation will ultimately be used for our good.

But if God allows us to go through temptation,
does that mean He is trying to get us to sin? If we
had no choice but to sin, the answer would be yes.
But Paul wrote: "No temptation has seized you
except what is common to man. And God is faithful: He will not let you be tempted beyond what
you can bear. But when you are tempted, He will
also provide a way out so that you can stand up
under it" (1 Corinthians 10:13).

When temptation comes, we can be certain that
God allowed it. He didn't send it, because Satan
is the source of temptation. If the temptation were
too great, God would have prevented Satan from
sending it. But God allowed it, knowing we have
the strength in Christ to handle it. That's another
reason to "count it pure joy."

Build Strength through Resistance

How does God use temptation to strengthen us?
"Because you know that the testing of your faith
develops perseverance. Perseverance must finish
its work so that you may be mature and complete
not lacking anything" (James 1:3-4).

When I was in eighth grade I went out for track.

I had never run track, but I thought it would be fairly easy. On the first day of practice, the coach had us run a mile. I thought, *There's nothing to this*.

Then he called us together and had us run wind sprints. Down the field we ran for a few hundred yards. When his whistle sounded we ran back up the field. Down and back, down and back—10 times. I was beginning to feel the strain.

But we weren't finished yet. Next he had us broad jump, throw the shot put, and the discus. When we finished with that, we ran another mile. Then we ran more wind sprints. We went through that cycle three times. And that was just the first day!

Each day for about the first week, the workouts got harder. My body felt like one giant ache. But gradually I began to build endurance. The more we worked out, the more strength and endurance I developed.

Medical science shows that when we start an exercise program, the old muscle tissue breaks down. Then new cells, and new blood vessels begin to form to nourish the cells. The more we exercise, the more muscle tissue and blood supply develop. Soon our increased endurance lets us do things physically that we never thought possible.

We build endurance to temptation in much the same way. The more we stand firm and make the right decisions, the stronger our spiritual lives become. Resisting temptation is sometimes painful. But when we resist, we grow stronger, so that one day we "may be mature and complete, not lacking anything" (James 1:4).

Recognize the Solution

"Count it pure joy" when you are tempted. Resist temptation. But try to overcome temptation in your own strength, and you're a dead duck! Jesus Christ is the *ultimate solution* to the temptation problem. Depend on His strength, not your own.

The same Bible verse that promises "Resist the devil and he will flee from you," begins with the instruction, "Submit yourselves then to God" (James 4:7). Only as we let Jesus control our lives will we have the strength to resist Satan.

Jesus can help us overcome temptation because He has faced it Himself. "Because He Himself suffered when He was tempted, He is able to help those who are being tempted" (Hebrews 2:18). "For we do not have a high priest who is unable to sympathize with our weaknesses, but we have one [Jesus] who has been tempted in every way, just as we are—yet was without sin" (Hebrews 4:15).

We should follow the example of the mouse who was being chased by a woman with a broom. He didn't keep his eye on the woman or the broom. He was too busy looking for his hole! Keep your eye on the Solution, Jesus, not on the temptation itself.

Refocus Attention

Another important step in overcoming temptation is to *refocus our attention*. James wrote, "Therefore, get rid of all moral filth and the evil that is so prevalent, and humbly accept the word planted in you, which can save you" (James 1:21).

We might say it this way today: "Get rid of the porno magazines and books. Be careful what you feed your mind through music, TV, and movies." In other words, quit filling your life with the things that lead to sin.

The second part of this verse (James 1:21) says to "accept the word planted in you." When tempted by Satan, Jesus overcame the attacks by using Scripture (Matthew 4:1-11). Each time Satan tempted Him, Jesus resisted by quoting a Scripture.

The psalmist wrote: "I have hidden Your Word in my heart that I might not sin against You" (Psalm 119:11). When temptation tries to pull us in the wrong direction, God's Word implanted in our minds and hearts will enable us to overcome Satan's attacks. (Praying and reading the Bible even 15-20 minutes a day, and memorizing 1 Bible verse each week, can give tremendous strength.)

Refocus Activity

One final word about overcoming temptation: We need to refocus our *activity* as well as our attention. Paul wrote to his young friend Timothy: "Flee the evil desires of youth and pursue righteousness, faith, love, and peace, along with those who call on the Lord out of a pure heart" (2 Timothy 2:22).

If we know that by going to a certain place, we will face a heavy temptation, maybe we shouldn't go. We don't overcome temptation by playing around with sin. Sometimes, said Paul, it's better just to stay out of the situation—if necessary, to turn tail and *run*.

Run to where? To those who "call on the Lord out of a pure heart" (v. 22). Refocusing our activity to include fellowship with other Christians is an important step in overcoming temptation. Such fellowship can provide tremendous strength and encouragement. It's easier to handle temptation when we have the support of Christian friends.

Sometimes, though, it comes down to you, the Lord, and the temptation. Then, staying out of sin is a matter of cold-blooded obedience.

James wrote, "Do not merely listen to the Word, and so deceive yourselves. Do what it says" (James 1:22). That may mean saying no to something your friends want you to do. It may mean giving up some habit in your life.

Whatever the Lord calls you to do, obey Him. Don't wait till it's convenient. Do it now. Refocusing your activity by obedience to Christ is sometimes hard. But it leads to freedom.

Feeling Free, Living Free

Bob Dylan recorded a song, "Gotta Serve Somebody," that describes a choice every person must make. "It may be the devil, or it might be the Lord," wrote Dylan, "but you're gonna have to serve somebody."

People like to think that by ignoring God and rejecting His way of life, they can be free. In reality, just the opposite is true. Without God, people are *slaves* of sin. They don't have the power *not* to sin.

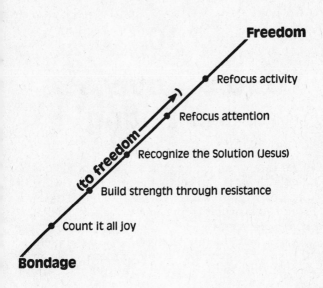

Paul wrote: "Don't you realize that you can choose your own master? You can choose sin (with death) or else obedience (with acquittal). The one to whom you offer yourself—he will take you and be your master and you will be his slave" (Romans 6:16, LB).

"Doing your own thing" really means doing the devil's thing. But letting Jesus Christ be Lord over your life brings true freedom.

"If the Son sets you free, you will be free indeed" (John 8:36).

10

Lord of Love, Sex, and Dating

Next time you pick up your school yearbook, take a good look at your class picture. If you were to cut 1 of every 10 girls out of that picture, the empty silhouettes would represent how many will become pregnant by high school graduation. If you cut one-half of your classmates out of the picture, that would show how many of their future marriages will end in divorce, based on current statistics.

Next to their need for Jesus Christ, the greatest need among high school students today is to have a right perspective on love, sex, and dating. Music, TV, and advertising saturate us with sexual messages. People have tossed around the word "love" till it has lost its meaning: "I love my stereo." "I love my car." "I love soccer." "I love John." "I love pickles and peanut butter." But we don't understand love or sex till we get to know the God who created them both.

Jesus Christ wants to be Lord of love, sex, and dating in our lives.

"I Love You If . . ."

Most dating relationships are one of three types. The first type might be called the "I-love-you-if" relationship: "I love you . . . if you will spend lots of money on me." "I love you if you will make out with me." "I love you if you will do what I want."

Hardly anyone would ever admit that his love depends on some "if." But it's an unstated part of many relationships. Such relationships end in disappointment and hurt because they are based entirely on selfishness.

"I Love You Because . . ."

A second kind of dating relationship might be called the "I-love-you-because" relationship: "I love you because you look beautiful." "I love you because you are captain of the junior tiddledy-winks team." "I love you because you are witty . . . or popular . . . or intelligent."

An I-love-you-because relationship may seem to be an improvement over the I-love-you-if kind. Perhaps it is. But it too is built on a shaky foundation.

For example: a couple is standing beside a locker at school. He is telling her how pretty she is and how much he loves her because she is so beautiful.

Suddenly "the new girl," the one who looks like a *Seventeen* model, walks by. She flashes her pearly whites at the boy by the locker, and he immediately forgets that his girlfriend is alive. His pupils dilate and lock onto the new girl as she makes her way down the hall. Meanwhile, his girlfriend is quiet, but there's a war going on inside her.

An I-love-you-because relationship produces insecurity. Like the I-love-you-if kind, it's *conditional:* "I love you because you are beautiful, or handsome, or whatever. But if something happened to you so that you no longer had this quality, or if I found someone who had more of it than you, I wouldn't love you anymore."

We live in a throw-away age. Even people have become throw-away items. And people are hurting because of cheap, shallow relationships.

"I Love You No Matter What"

The third kind of dating relationship is the "I-love-you-no-matter-what" kind: "I love you no matter what weaknesses I see in you." "I love you with all your imperfections." "I love you just the way you are."

No-matter-what love is especially important in marriage. But it can be the basis of dating relationships too. In marriage, no-matter-what love means loving someone "for better or for worse," "for as long as we both shall live."

In a dating relationship, no-matter-what love means you are in the relationship to *give*, not just to get. It means that, even when you break up or date other people, you can still be friends, because you want what's best for the other person.

The kinds of dating relationships we experience play an important part in determining what our marriages will be like. If we only experience *conditional* relationships while dating, it's hard to turn on no-matter-what love when we marry. Whatever character qualities have been built into our lives, whatever we have learned about relationships— that's what we take into a marriage.

We don't see a lot of dating relationships based on no-matter-what love. The reason is that most people are not plugged into the source, Jesus Christ.

Jesus' life on earth is the ultimate example of no-matter-what love. He laid down His life to show what real love is. And three days later He picked it up so that *we* could have the ability to love.

Jesus Christ holds the key to successful love life. Not only does He love you "no matter what," but He can love others with that kind of love— *through you*.

"How can we know if we really love each other?" "How should we express our love?" "What about sex?" For the answers to these and other questions, check out 1 Corinthians 13. When we love with Jesus' love, the qualities described in this chapter of the Bible will establish the pattern for our dating relationships.

Patient

Love is patient (1 Corinthians 13:4). In other words, love is not in a hurry. How many times have you seen couples meet, start dating, and almost immediately get involved in a deep physical and emotional relationship? That kind of relationship usually explodes, leaving two hurt people.

Why does it happen that way? Because things get too heavy too fast. Real love is willing not to hurry. Real love is patient. It takes time to get to know the other person.

How much do you really know about the person you are dating? Is he or she lazy, neat, honest? How much of what you see in your date is a charade acted out just to impress you?

Are you objective about interpreting his or her actions? For example, if your date lies to her parents in order to be with you, do you interpret that action as proof of her love for you? Or do you see it as an indication that she might lie to you too?

Love is patient. It takes the time needed to get to know the other person and to develop a solid relationship.

Another way love demonstrates patience is by *accepting* the other person, rather than trying to fit him or her into a mold. Someone who is patient doesn't try to change the other person.

Before Carol and I married, she wore contact lenses. But shortly after we got married, she started wearing glasses all the time. That irritated me. The more she wore the glasses, the more irritated I became. And the more I got irritated, the more Carol wore the glasses.

Finally I prayed, "Lord, it's obvious that I'm not making much progress in changing my wife's mind about those glasses. If her mind is going to be changed, You are going to have to change it. I give this irritation up to You. I'm going to accept Carol just as she is, even if she starts wearing those glasses to bed!"

About four weeks later, Carol was looking in the mirror when she said, "You know, I would look a lot better if I wore contacts. But the ones I have now hurt my eyes. That's why I quit wearing them.

Do you think we could get some of those soft lenses and see if they will work?"

"I think we could probably work that out," I replied.

Love is patient. It doesn't get in a hurry and it doesn't try to jam the other person into a mold.

Kind

Love is kind (1 Corinthians 13:4). Real love looks for ways to help the other person be the best he or she can be. It is creatively helpful.

Some people would never believe it, but there is more to do on a date than make out. If a relationship centers on the physical aspect, how *kind* is it? Is such a relationship helping either person become the best he or she can be?

If you really care, look for creative things to do on a date—activities that will benefit the other person. For example:

• *Study together.* Chances are, both you and your date could use some support in this area.

• *Exercise together.* Help each other stay in shape by jogging together, playing tennis, etc.

• *Share Christ together.* Pray with your date that God will give you an opportunity to tell another couple about Him. Consider arranging a double date for that purpose.

Most people wouldn't think of this as a dating activity. But it is a great way to spend an evening, and to grow together in the Lord.

• *Develop a ministry to others.* Find someone who needs your help (at an old folks' home or jail, for example). Then discover ways to have a ministry with that person.

• *Make a commitment to pray together at the beginning and end of every date.* This may sound weird, but it's a great way to keep your relationship on the right track.

Praying together helps develop the spiritual side of your relationship. It also helps you avoid too much physical involvement. Somehow it's easier to stay away from "Passion Pit" when you start and end a date by talking with God.

"Love is kind" when a relationship breaks up too. Some couples who think they are madly in love one week, hate each other the next week. One week they are saying, "Oh, we're *so* in love!" The following week they are saying of each other, "What a creep! He is the biggest jerk I've ever known." But a dating relationship that includes kindness—building up the other person—can end in friendship instead of bitterness and hurt.

Real love is kind.

Not Jealous or Boastful

Love is not jealous or boastful (1 Corinthians 13:4).

A jealous person is a *possessive* person. Have you ever watched a possessive girl with her boyfriend? The two of them are walking down the hall at school, and she has his arm in a vise grip. No way is she going to let him get loose—unless, possibly, some other girl looks his way. Then the jealous girlfriend might let the guy out of her clutches, just long enough to claw the other girl's eyes out!

Real love knows that people need a variety of

relationships. If you really care, you will be willing for the other person to develop friendships apart from you. You will even be willing for him or her to date other people, if doing so seems best for the person you care about.

Real love is not jealous. Neither is it *boastful*. It doesn't make you try to impress the other person by acting like someone you're not.

People try to impress each other with the clothes they wear, the money they spend, the way they act. Girls try to look like sex symbols. Guys come on like macho men. The problem is that, at some point, the masks have to come off. Real love is based on honesty. So why try to be someone you're not?

A good way to avoid phoniness in a relationship is to make a commitment to yourself: "Right from the start of this relationship, I am going to be honest. I am not going to try to impress anyone by acting like someone I'm not. I am going to be real. If my date likes the real me, great. If not, at least we won't build a relationship on something that's false."

Not Proud

Love is not proud (1 Corinthians 13:4). It does not have an inflated idea of its own importance.

Several years ago, my wife Carol and I went to Hawaii. We had been looking forward to a romantic time—swaying palms, moonlit walks on the beach. Instead, we got to Hawaii and had one of the biggest fights we had ever had. The reason? I was being prideful. I was determined to do what

I wanted to do no matter what.

Some guys think that a girlfriend is supposed to be their slave, catering to every selfish whim. Some girls get the idea that a boyfriend should bend over backward to please them. In a godly relationship, both parties look for ways to serve the other person, rather than pridefully expecting to be served.

Not Self-seeking

Love is not self-seeking (1 Corinthians 13:5). It doesn't insist on its own way. Real love does not take selfish advantage of anyone. Someone who really cares does not allow sexual desire to overcome his concern for the other person. A person who really cares doesn't say "I love you" when what he really means is "I want to *use* you to satisfy my desires."

Here we go again, someone is thinking, *more "sex-is-bad" propaganda*.

If there are some "don'ts" associated with the Christian view of sex, it's not because sex is bad. In fact, God is fired up about sex. He is for it. After all, He made it.

Suppose I have a friend who is a watchmaker. He gives me a watch as a gift. But no sooner does He give it to me than I put it on my foot and start jumping up and down. My watchmaker friend yells, "Don't!" Why? Because he made the watch, and he knows how it is supposed to be used.

God made sex. He understands it. He has given it to us as a gift. When He says don't, it's because He doesn't want us to abuse His gift. He wants the gift of sex to be the very best for us that it can be. And He knows that sex is only what it should be when it is used the way He designed it to be used.

God's design for sex is that, in marriage, two people should come together as *one*. Jesus said: "At the beginning of creation God 'made them male and female.' 'For this reason a man will leave his father and mother and be united to his wife, and the two will become one flesh.' So they are no longer two, but one. Therefore what God has joined together, let man not separate" (Mark 10:6-9).

The Apostle Paul had this "one flesh" truth in mind when he wrote: "Sexual sin is never right. Our bodies were not made for that, but for the Lord, and the Lord wants to fill our bodies with Himself. And God is going to raise our bodies from the dead by His power just as He raised up the Lord Jesus Christ.

"Don't you realize that your bodies are actually members of Christ? So should I take part of Christ and join Him to a prostitute? Never! And don't you know that if a man joins himself to a prostitute she becomes a part of him and he becomes a part of her? For God tells us in the Scripture that in His sight the two become one person" (1 Corinthians 6:13-16, LB).

God's design for sex is that two people be joined as one, not only in the physical sense, but also in their total personalities. God designed sex to be an expression of *oneness*—physical, emotional, and spiritual oneness. When people get involved in sex outside of marriage, it's like they are leaving part of their personalities with their sexual part-

ners. Both partners are losing—and stealing—
something precious.

God's "don'ts" regarding sex are an expression
of His love. He wants His gift of sex to provide
joy and fulfillment. He wants us to discipline ourselves before marriage in order to enjoy maximum
fulfillment in marriage.

Someone who really cares for another person is
willing to discipline his own sexual desires. He
wants the best for the other person, so he doesn't
selfishly misuse the gift of sex. Real love is not
self-seeking.

Beating the Odds

Half of the people reading this book can count on
being divorced—if they follow the general population trends. But that doesn't have to happen.
With Jesus in control, Christians can beat the odds.

As we develop the qualities of real love,
1 Corinthians 13 love, we can look forward to successful dating and marriage relationships. Let's
learn "no-matter-what love" while we are still dating—before selfishness causes broken marriages
and families. Let's let Jesus be Lord of love, sex,
and dating in our lives.

*"Love is patient, love is kind. It does not envy,
it does not boast, it is not proud. It is not rude,
it is not self-seeking, it is not easily angered, it
keeps no record of wrongs. Love does not delight
in evil but rejoices with the truth. It always pro-
tects, always trusts, always hopes, always per-
severes. Love never fails" (1 Corinthians 13:4-8).*

11
Lord of Character

Happiness is . . .

"A good bank account, a good cook, and good digestion."

> —Jean-Jacques Rousseau

"The absence of pain."

> —Chinese proverb

"A way-station between too little and too much."

> —Channing Pollock

"The only ones among you who will be really happy are those who will have sought and found how to serve."

> —Albert Schweitzer

"Happiness is but a name."

> —Robert Burns

*"The strength and the happiness of a man con-
sists in finding out the way in which God is going,
and going in that way too."*
—Henry Ward Beecher

*"It's pretty hard to tell what does bring hap-
piness; poverty and wealth have both failed."*
—Kin Hubbard

*"Happiness is neither within us only, or with-
out us; it is the union of ourselves with God."*
—Pascal

What does happiness mean to you? A good job?
A new car? Friends? New clothes?

Jesus Christ's formula for happiness is recorded
in Matthew 5. The ingredients are called the "Beatitudes." In them Jesus gives eight character
qualities that describe the happy person.

Actually He uses the word *blessed*. It's a word
that means happy, but it's not the kind of happiness most people understand. The kind of happiness Jesus described is not based on
circumstances—making money, winning games,
or having lots of dates. It's a gut-level kind of happiness that grows out of a relationship with God.

A lot of people, even church people, don't take
Jesus' formula for happiness seriously. That's because it includes instructions like these: Start by
being poor in spirit. Add a pint of mourning and
a quart of meekness. Be hungry, merciful, and pure
in heart. Make peace. And rejoice when you are
persecuted!

In short, Jesus' formula for happiness turns the
world's values upside down. But here they are—

eight character qualities that Jesus wants to develop in you—our Lord's formula for happy living.

Wealthy Poverty

"Blessed are the poor in spirit, for theirs is the kingdom of heaven" (Matthew 5:3).

I was jogging in a light rain one afternoon when I came across a pitiful sight. A middle-aged man slouched under a dripping billboard. He was unshaven, dressed in rags, and his shoes were riddled with holes. I nodded to him as I passed.

About a hundred yards down the road, I began to feel that I should go back and talk with the man. As I approached him I noticed another billboard nearby, sponsored by a local church. It read: "Let Jesus Untie the Knots!"

"Have you ever seen that sign before?" I asked the man.

"Yeah, I guess I have," he answered.

"Have you ever thought much about it?" I asked.

"No."

I found out that his name was Charles. He had no family, no home, no job. He had been living in the woods in a nearby park, sleeping under a tree. Every so often he visited a blood bank where he exchanged a pint of his blood for money to buy food.

He hadn't done much of anything with his life. He had no accomplishments, nothing to look back on with pride. But when I began to talk to him about receiving Christ, he was ready.

"I've tried everything else," Charles responded. "It wouldn't hurt to try Him, would it?"

I prayed, and asked Charles to pray after me. Tears began to stream down his face. He pulled a dirty old bandanna out of his pocket and wiped away the rain and tears.

After we had finished praying I asked Charles if he had received Jesus into his life. He looked at me with new sparkle in his eyes and a big smile on his face. And he said, "Yeah, I really did!"

I believe a miracle took place that day in Charles' life. I also believe that one of the main reasons it happened was because Charles recognized his need. He was poor physically. But also he was in a condition which the Bible calls being "poor in spirit."

One of the biggest obstacles that keeps people away from God is the attitude that they are OK without Him. Because they make good grades, or have good looks, or their family is wealthy, they figure they don't need God. They feel it's alright for some hard-luck drifter like Charles to realize he's needy, but not them. Such an attitude is the opposite of being "poor in spirit."

Jesus placed this ingredient at the beginning of the list for a reason. Being poor in spirit is absolutely necessary in order to develop the other seven character qualities. Only by recognizing our need for Christ, and letting Him control our lives, can we become like Him in character.

Happy Grief

"Blessed are those who mourn, for they will be comforted" (Matthew 5:4).

God doesn't want us to be negative, sour people. But He does want us to be concerned, even heartbroken, about some things.

The week that Jesus was crucified, He entered the city of Jerusalem with His disciples. As they came in sight of the beautiful temple and its surrounding buildings, the disciples marveled at the magnificent architecture.

When the disciples saw the city, they were excited by its beauty. But Jesus, seeing the same sights, was concerned about the *people* of Jerusalem: "But as they came closer to Jerusalem and He saw the city ahead, He began to cry. 'Eternal peace was within your reach and you turned it down,' He wept, 'and now it is too late'" (Luke 19:41-42, LB).

A lot of people today look at our messed-up world and say, "I don't give a rip, just as long as I'm getting along OK." When Jesus saw people hurting, when He saw injustice, when He saw moral corruption, it grieved Him. He wept over it.

It ought to concern us to know that people are dying of hunger. It should concern us that evil people are taking advantage of the weak and helpless.

Most of all, we should be grieved about the sin in ourselves. One sure sign of the Holy Spirit's work in our lives is a sensitivity to sins we have committed.

Unless we become concerned about sin, both in the world and in our own hearts, we will never know the "happiness" that God intends for us to have. Jesus wept over the sins of the world. As He develops His character in us, we will grieve over sins too.

One way to begin developing this character quality is by asking God to help us see the world and ourselves from *His* perspective. Dr. Robert Pierce, who helped establish orphanages, missions, hospitals, leprosariums, and sanitariums across the world, wrote a prayer in the front of his Bible. It says, "Let my heart be broken by the things that break the heart of God." God wants us to share His heartache for a world that is dying as a result of its sin and rebellion.

Gentle Strength

"Blessed are the meek, for they will inherit the earth" (Matthew 5:5).

Being meek doesn't mean being namby-pamby or weak. Meekness is best demonstrated by someone who is strong but who has his strength, along with his emotions, his feelings, and his desires, under control. Meekness is like a wild horse that's been tamed enough to ride, but whose strong, free spirit has not been broken.

If there is one character quality that the American student needs today, it is this kind of meekness—this self-discipline. Our society seems to be producing fewer and fewer people who are willing to do something hard or unpleasant just because it is *right*.

Our lack of self-discipline shows itself in our selfish desire for things, our lust, and our pride. We want what we want when we want it.

God is looking for people who are willing to say, "Lord, everything I have belongs to You. My money, my possessions, my personality, my body—

everything I have is Yours to use." Only when we are willing to make that commitment will we develop the character quality of meekness.

Contented Hunger

"Blessed are those who hunger and thirst for righteousness, for they will be filled" (Matthew 5:6).

My drifter friend Charles got hungry enough to sell his own blood for food. God wants us to hunger for Him like that.

We have life so easy today that it's hard to appreciate what it means to be hungry. Most of our refrigerators are bulging with food. We can have almost anything we want to eat. But when a person is really hungry, it's nearly impossible to keep his mind off food. Likewise, when we are hungry for God, we think of Him often. We want to be with Him, to fellowship with Him.

The psalmist wrote: "O God, You are my God, earnestly I seek You; my soul thirsts for You, my body longs for You, in a dry and weary land where there is no water" (Psalm 63:1). "As the deer pants for streams of water, so my soul pants for You, O God. My soul thirsts for God, for the living God" (Psalm 42:1-2).

The opposite of this kind of hunger after God is the problem of *apathy*. Many people just don't care about knowing the Lord. Or they don't care enough to do anything about it.

The antidote for spiritual apathy is to see God as He really is. When we really see God, we begin to hunger after Him. It's like my friend Bryan said one night while we were jogging together—"You know, Barry, the more I see Christ working in my life, the more I desire Him."

A practical way to develop this character quality is to spend time alone with God in prayer and in the Bible. As we learn to fellowship with God, our spiritual hunger will grow. And Jesus promises that those who hunger and thirst for righteousness *will be filled*.

Forgiven Forgivers

"Blessed are the merciful, for they will be shown mercy" (Matthew 5:7).

Almost every week I talk to some young person about his relationship with parents, or brothers and sisters, or teachers, or some other person. And I meet a lot of people who are resentful, bitter, and unwilling to forgive.

Jesus said: "If you forgive men when they sin against you, your heavenly Father will also forgive you. But if you do not forgive men their sins, your Father will not forgive your sins" (Matthew 6:14-15).

A "merciful" person is one who shows compassion to others and who forgives them even when they don't deserve it. Developing this character quality begins when a person understands how much it cost God to forgive him. And a person grows in mercy as he learns to forgive others.

It takes a certain amount of courage to tell a person "I forgive you." It's risky because that same person could hurt us again. But that's exactly how God deals with us. He forgives us even though

He knows we aren't perfect people and might commit the same sin again.

20/20 Heart-sight

"Blessed are the pure in heart, for they will see God" (Matthew 5:8).

This may be the most difficult of the beatitudes because it seems impossible to live up to. Is Jesus saying that only the person who never has any impure thoughts or desires will make it to heaven? If so, heaven may have a very sparse population!

In Jewish culture, to "see the face" of someone important or to be "in his presence" were terms that expressed great *favor*. In those days before TV, it was considered an honor just to *see* a king or queen.

So, when Jesus said that the pure in heart will "see God," He probably was not referring just to heaven. The pure in heart will be favored *now*, as well as in heaven, by being in God's presence, knowing Him, and understanding His will for them.

The expression "pure as gold" is helpful in understanding the phrase "pure in heart." Gold is most valuable when it has few impurities. A person who is pure in heart is someone whose *mind*, *motives*, and *desires* are not mixed with a lot of impurities.

Though it's not the only area involved, when we think of impurity we usually think of the sexual area. Imagine someone spending a lot of money to sod his lawn. Beautiful grass covers the yard as a result, and it looks great. But imagine someone

taking a shovel full of that new sod and dumping
it on the living room carpet. "Beautiful" is hardly
the word you would use to describe how that
would look.

In a similar way, sex in marriage—within the
boundaries of a lifelong commitment—is a blessing of God. It's beautiful. But sex outside of marriage is like dirt on the living room carpet—dirty
and damaging. Saving sex till God provides the
right marriage partner is one aspect of being pure.

Sexual purity in our thought life is another problem for most people. Visual stimulation reaches
our minds through the things we see and read. It's
inevitable. But what matters is how we handle
those thoughts. As Martin Luther said, "You cannot stop the birds from flying over your head, but
you can stop them from nesting in your hair."

How do we develop the character quality of a
pure heart? Psalm 119:9 instructs us: "How can a
young man keep his way pure? By living according to Your Word." The Apostle Paul wrote, "Do
not conform any longer to the pattern of this world,
but be transformed by the renewing of your mind"
(Romans 12:1).

Another passage dealing with purity is found in
1 John: "If we walk in the light as He is in the
light, we have fellowship with one another, and
the blood of Jesus, His Son, purifies us from every
sin. If we claim to be without sin, we deceive
ourselves and the truth is not in us. If we confess
our sins, He is faithful and just and will forgive us
our sins and purify us from all unrighteousness"
(1 John 1:7-9).

How to get a pure heart? *(1) Get into God's
Word, the Bible. (2) Allow Jesus Christ to trans-*

form you by "renewing your mind," so that you think His thoughts. (3) When you do sin, don't cover it up or try to excuse yourself. Instead, confess it to God and ask for forgiveness. He promises not only to forgive but to "purify" you "from all unrighteousness."

As Jesus purifies you, like gold being refined of impurities, you will see God in a new light. You will know Him better and understand His plan for your life.

Peaceful Warriors

"Blessed are the peacemakers, for they will be called sons of God" (Matthew 5:9).

I guess if there is one sin that is most common among young people it's the tendency to cut down other people. But Jesus said, "Blessed are the peacemakers, for they will be called sons of God" (Matthew 5:9).

Notice that Jesus didn't say blessed are the "peace lovers." Sometimes we think that the way to be a peacemaker is to live and let live. But a peacemaker is not someone who just minds his own business and tries not to offend anyone.

I remember times when friends have confronted me about things they saw in my life that shouldn't have been there. Such confrontation took courage. It involved the risk that I might say, "It's none of your business." But my friends were peacemakers. They were concerned about me. And they felt that, in the long run, confronting me with the problem would be best for me.

A peacemaker is one who brings people together. Sometimes saying nothing, living and letting live, keeps people apart—from other people and from God. A good way to determine whether you are a peacemaker is to ask, "If I knew that a problem existed between myself and someone else, would I be willing to go to that person and try to resolve the problem?"

Being a peacemaker may mean saying, "I was wrong. Will you forgive me?" A peacemaker is one who becomes part of the solution rather than ignoring the problem.

Losers That Win

"Blessed are those who are persecuted because of righteousness, for theirs is the kingdom of heaven. Blessed are you when people insult you, persecute you and falsely say all kinds of evil against you because of Me. Rejoice and be glad, because great is your reward in heaven, for in the same way they persecuted the prophets who were before you" (Matthew 5:10-12).

Imagine what it must have been like living as a Christian in the first century. Thousands of believers were hunted down and killed. Others lost their jobs, their social standings, their homes.

Christians were fed to lions. They were burned at the stake. They were branded and tortured. Some were sewn inside animal skins, then attacked by hungry dogs. Nero, the emperor of Rome, is believed to have lit his gardens at night by covering Christians with pitch, placing them on crosses, and setting them on fire.

Even today, Christians in some countries risk their lives in order to stand up for Jesus Christ. Yet many of us are afraid to stand up for Him on the campus and at work.

Jesus said that those who live under His lordship can have joy when they face persecution. That joy comes from looking beyond the difficult circumstances to the *blessings* that result from persecution.

Peter wrote to some Christians who had been driven from their homes because of their commitment to Christ: "These trials are only to test your faith, to see whether or not it is strong and pure. It is being tested as fire tests gold and purifies it— and your faith is far more precious to God than mere gold; so if your faith remains strong after being tried in the test tube of fiery trials, it will bring you much praise and glory and honor on the day of His return" (1 Peter 1:7, LB).

James, also writing to Christians who were being persecuted for their faith, reminded them: "Dear brothers, is your life full of difficulties and temptations? Then be happy, for when the way is rough, your patience has a chance to grow. So let it grow, and don't try to squirm out of your problems. For when your patience is finally in full bloom, then you will be ready for anything, strong in character, full and complete" (James 1:2-4, LB).

What made those first-century Christians willing to suffer and die? How could they have joy while being ripped off and beaten up?

I believe it was because they really *knew* Jesus Christ and understood how to live under His lordship. They understood that "present sufferings are not worth comparing with the glory that will be revealed in us" (Romans 8:18). They had a joy that did not depend on circumstances.

How do you develop this character quality? Start "laying your life down" for Jesus Christ—especially at school. Demonstrate such a loyalty to Him that those who reject Jesus will also reject you.

Formula for happiness: Start by being poor in spirit. Add a pint of mourning and a quart of meekness. Be hungry, merciful, and pure in heart. Make peace. And rejoice when you are persecuted! True happiness comes from living under the lordship of Jesus Christ—and letting Him reproduce His character in you.

12

Lord of All

I was convinced that my 1963 Oldsmobile "Ninety-eight" reeked with class. Everybody else just thought it reeked.

But I liked it. So what if it was nearly 20 years old and colored a blotchy gray? So what if it only had three hubcaps, and the backseat was full of mildew? So what if the hood had a huge crease where a tree had fallen on it? The car felt comfortable to me, like an old pair of jeans.

Then one sad day I drove it to the Atlanta airport and parked it. When I tried to start it again, the car was dead. I don't mean it had a dead battery. The old car had expired. I sold it for eight dollars.

But suppose that someone had walked up to me in that airport parking lot and said, "Hey buddy, I've wanted a car like yours for a long time. I'll trade you even, your car for my brand new Datsun 280 Z."

Suppose I had replied, "Well, it's true that my car won't run. But it does have three good hub-

137

caps. And the doors work really well ... Nah, I think I'll just hold on to it."

That's how a lot of us respond to Jesus. He offers an exchange too—His life for ours. Too often we make the mistake of holding on to our lives when He wants to give us a brand new life. What Jesus wants is a total exchange, a trade—His life for ours.

The Apostle Paul described that exchange: "I have been crucified with Christ and I no longer live, but Christ lives in me. The life I live in the body, I live by faith in the Son of God, who loved me and gave Himself for me" (Galatians 2:20).

We are saved by trusting in Christ, salvation is a free gift. But we only experience the *quality* of life God wants for us as we let Jesus be Lord of all. That involves an exchange—giving ourselves completely to the Lord so that He can live through us. That is total commitment.

A Total Exchange

A young man came to Jesus one day and asked Him a question: "Good Teacher, what must I do to inherit eternal life?" (Mark 10:17)

I don't think he just wanted to know how to get to heaven when he died. He wanted to know how to have a *quality* life, one that goes on forever but which begins in this life. He wanted to know how to have the kind of life that Jesus offered when He said, "I am come that they might have life and that they might have it more abundantly" (John 10:10, KJV).

Jesus answered the young man, "You know the

commandments: 'Do not murder, do not commit adultery, do not steal, do not give false testimony, do not defraud, honor your father and mother.'"

The young man replied, "Teacher, all these I have kept since I was a boy."

"Jesus looked at him and loved him. 'One thing you lack,' He said. 'Go, sell everything you have and give to the poor, and you will have treasure in heaven. Then come, follow Me'" (Mark 10:19-21).

This young man must have lived an outstanding moral life. He probably went to synagogue every Sabbath and the neighbors talked about what a "nice kid" he was. But Jesus saw that he had a problem. Jesus told him, "One thing you lack." Just one thing. . . .

Picture an expensive stereo. All of the components are the best—50-inch speakers, tape deck for cassette and 8-track, plus the finest of turntables. The stereo system has a 100+ watt receiver that operates with only .01 percent harmonic distortion. This stereo has all the finest equipment for recording and listening to music, but one thing is lacking. The electrical cord lies on the floor, six feet away from the nearest electrical outlet.

The stereo looks good, but in its present condition, it is useless. Why? It is not plugged in to the power source.

Sometimes to lack just one thing is to lack the most important thing. That was the case with the rich young man. He looked good on the outside. He had learned to follow the rules. But Christianity is a relationship, not a bunch of rules.

The rich young man was not willing to let go of his life—to exchange it for Jesus' life. As a result,

"He went away sad, because he had great wealth" (Mark 10:22).

The point of the rich young ruler's story is not that everyone should get rid of their material possessions. The point is that Jesus wants all of us— not just our church attendance, or our money, or our good deeds. He wants *us*.

Some people approach Christianity as if they were bargain hunting. They want to know, "How much can I get away with and still be a Christian? Can I smoke, and drink, and have sex, and still be saved?" Those people are missing the point. They don't really understand what a relationship with Jesus is all about.

Possess Nothing, Own Everything

The rich young ruler flunked the test. He was not willing to make the total exchange. Another Bible character, Abraham, faced a similar test.

God promised to give Abraham a son. But Abraham and his wife Sarah remained childless for many years after that promise was made. Finally, when Abraham and Sarah were past the age of childbearing, Sarah miraculously gave birth to a son, Isaac.

God had also promised to make Abraham's descendants a great nation. Since Isaac was Abraham's only son, he was the key to the fulfillment of that promise. This special son, born in Abraham's old age, must have been greatly loved by his father.

Then one day God spoke again to Abraham. He asked Abraham to take Isaac to the top of Mount

Moriah and sacrifice him there on an altar (Genesis 22). Early the next morning, Abraham woke Isaac and they set out for the mountain.

When they got there, Abraham built the altar and prepared to offer the sacrifice—his only son, the one he had waited years for. Only a parent can understand the anguish Abraham must have felt.

As Abraham drew back the knife to plunge it into Isaac's heart, God stopped him at the last moment. Abraham found a ram caught in a nearby thicket and sacrificed it instead, as God had planned for him to do.

Abraham was willing to give up the most precious thing in his life. Unlike the rich young ruler, Abraham didn't hold onto anything. He gave everything up to God. And as a result, God blessed him.

I have a son too. So Abraham's story has a lot of meaning to me. My son Scott is quite active, and I used to worry a lot about his safety. Buses barreled down our street, and I used to have a terrible fear that Scott might be run over. I remember thinking, *If anything happened to that boy, I don't think I could bear it*.

Then one day I read the story of Abraham and began to ask myself if I really trusted God with my son. Would I be able to give up Scott if God asked me to do that?

I remembered a quotation I had heard once: "He who possesses nothing owns everything." I realized that if I would place "on the altar" all the things that were precious to me, I would then be able to fully appreciate and enjoy the things God allowed me to keep.

That day, I knelt and surrendered my son Scott.

I prayed, "Lord, You can have him if You want him. He is Yours. You may do what You desire. Scott is Yours." As I prayed that prayer, God gave me a tremendous sense of peace and freedom. My excessive fear for Scott's safety was gone. And within a week, the buses that ran by our house were routed another way!

Gain Through Losing

For the rich young man, it was wealth that kept him from letting Jesus be Lord of his life. What is it for you? If Jesus were to say to you, "Give up all that you have and follow Me," what would make you hold back?

It might be something that is going on with a girlfriend or boyfriend that needs to stop. It might be some relationship or habit. It might be some form of entertainment that keeps filling your mind with garbage thoughts. It might be guilt, or a bad attitude, or a broken relationship. It might be that you are trying to be a "part-time Christian"—turning on religion on Sundays, then turning it off the rest of the week.

Whatever it is that makes you hold back, it puts you in the same position as that rich young man. Jesus told him, "You lack one thing."

On January 8, 1956 in the jungles of Ecuador, five young men were killed by Auca tribesmen, primitive Indians to whom these men were trying to bring the Gospel. One of the young men was Jim Elliot. Before his death, Jim had written in his journal: "He is no fool who gives what he cannot keep to gain what he cannot lose."

Life is short. In the long run, success will not be measured in dollars and cents, or by the number of friends we have, or by what team records we set. Success will be measured by how we have responded to Jesus Christ. We are truly successful and spiritually fulfilled when we allow Jesus Christ to be Lord of all.

The Journey

In his classic book *Pilgrim's Progress*, John Bunyan described a journey. The journey began for the main character, Pilgrim, the day he received Jesus as his Saviour.

This book you are reading now has described the beginning of that journey. None of us really begins the Christian life till we have been properly introduced to Jesus, as discussed in the earlier chapters.

Once the burden of his sin was lifted, Pilgrim began a journey to Celestial City, or heaven. This book has described some of what is involved in making that journey—the problems to be faced, the questions to be answered.

The journey involves learning what God thinks is important and making His priorities ours. The journey involves getting to know Jesus better and better as He builds His character in us. We make progress in the journey as we let Jesus be Lord of every area of our lives—Lord of our attitudes; Lord over temptation; Lord of love, sex, and dating; Lord of all.

Jesus *is* Lord. One day everyone will acknowledge it (Philippians 2:10-11). One day everything will belong to Him. The happiest, wisest choice you could ever make is to let Him be Lord of your life now.

You can make that choice by praying, "Lord, here is my life. It belongs to You. As far as I understand, everything about myself belongs to You. You are my Lord."

P.S. Making the decision to follow Christ on a daily basis is tough sometimes. Hopefully this book has been a help. But if you want to explore some of the issues in more depth, or if you want some other resources that will challenge you, then write me: Barry St. Clair, 3117 Majestic Circle, Avondale Estates, Georgia 30002. Let's talk it over—because I'm convinced that Jesus wants to change your life and use you to make an impact on the world!